General Aptitude

(CSIR NET – Previous Q & A with explanation and hint to solve)

(For all Competitive Exam- Specially CSIR-NET, DBT, ICMR, GATE etc.)

Pradip Kumar Ray

<u>Surrender</u>

All the CSIR-NET , GATE, DBT aspirant and future generations of me and them and of course the readers of my book.

Pradip Kumar Ray, Burdwan.

My word

The aim of this book is to focus on important topics according to new trends of various competitive exams such as CSIR-NET, DBT, GATE, SET etc. Aptitude section has a major role irrespective of subject stream. This book has prepared on previous questions asked on CSIR-NET exam. All the answers have mentioned along with explanation and note to solve these problems. The Hint to solve the questions will help the students. The tips and tricks have also explained nicely. This is my hope and I am confirmed about the fact that this book will help the students to understand the problem with tips and tricks.

Pradip Kumar Ray,

223-A.B.Mukherjee Road,

Nutanganj, Dighirpool, Bardhhaman – 713102.

<u>My gratitude and acknowledgment</u>

To complete this book I have taken help from various books, magazines, websites, social media such as YouTube, Quora, discussions with different scholars and their various opinions, various conventional books, etc. My sincere gratitude to all of them and to the publisher of this book. These will help to increase the practical knowledge of the reader.

Pradip Kumar Ray.

Refresh Your Memory and have a look on Note before solving

Number System

Number System is divided into 4 parts:

- Classification
- Divisibility Test
- Division and Remainder Rules
- Sum Rules

Types	Description
Natural Numbers	All counting numbers (1, 2, 3, 4, 5....∞)
Whole Numbers	Natural number +zero (0, 1, 2, 3, 4, 5...∞)
Integers	All whole numbers including Negative number +Positive number (∞.......-4,-3,-2,-1,0,1,2,3,4,5....∞)
Even & Odd Numbers	All whole number divisible by 2 is Even (0,2,4,6,8,10,12.....∞) andwhichdoesnot divideby2areOdd(1,3,5,7,9,11,13,15, 17,19....∞)
Prime Numbers	Itcanbepositiveornegativeexcept1,ifthenumber is not divisible by any number except the number itself.(2,3,5,7,11,13,17,19,23,29,31,37,41,43, 47,53,59,61....∞)
Composite Numbers	Natural numbers which are not prime.
Co-Prime	Twonaturalnumberaandbaresaidtobeco-primeiftheirHCFis1.

Numbers	IFA Number
Divisible by 2	End with 0,2,4,6,8 are divisible by 2
Divisible by 3	Sum of its digits is divisible by 3
Divisible by 4	Last two digit divisible by 4

Divisible by 5	Ends with 0 or 5
Divisible by 6	Divides by Both 2 & 3
Divisible by 8	Last3digitdivideby8
Divisible by 10	End with 0
Divisible by 11	[Sum of its digit in odd places-Sum of its digits in even places]=0 or multiple of 11
Divisible by 12	[The number must be divisible by 3 and 4]
Divisible by 13	[Multiply last digit with 4 and add it to remaining number in given number, result must be divisible by 13]
Divisible by 14	[The number must be divisible by 2 and 7. Because 2 and 7 are prime factors of 14.]
Divisible by 15	[The number should be divisible by 3 and 5. Because 3 and 5 are prime factors of 15.]
Divisible by 16	[The number formed by last four digits in given number must be divisible by 16.]
Divisible by 17	[Multiply last digit with 5 and subtract. It from remaining number in given number, result must be divisible by 17]
Divisible by 18	[The number should be divisible by 2 and 9]
Divisible by 19	[Multiply last digit with 2 and add it to remaining number in given number, result must be divisible by 19]
Divisible by 20	[The number formed by last two digits in given number must be divisible by 20.]

Divisible by 24 – If a number is divisible by 3 and 8 both, then it will also be divisible by 14 as well.

Example – 4848 is divisible by 3 and 8 both, so it will be divisible by 24 also.

Divisible by 40 – If a number is divisible by 5 and 8 both, then it will also be divisible by 40 as well.
Example – 8080 is divisible by 5 and 8 both, so it will be divisible by 40 also.

Divisible by 80 – If a number is divisible by 5 and 16 both, then it will also be divisible by 80 as well.
Example – 80160 is divisible by 5 and 16 both, so it will be divisible by 80 also.

Some important properties of Numbers:

1. The number 1 is neither prime nor composite.

2. The only number which is even is 2.

3. All the prime numbers greater than 3 can be written in the form of (6k+1) or (6k-1) where k is an integer.

4. Square of every natural number can be written in the form 3n or (3n+1) and 4n or (4n+1).

5. The tens digit of every perfect square is even unless the square is ending in 6 in which case the tens digit is odd.

6. The product of n consecutive natural numbers is always divisible by n!, where n!= 1X2X3X4X....Xn (known as factorial n).

BODMAS rule

B   Bracket (Brackets are solved in order of (), {} and [] respectively.
O   Order (Powers, Square Roots, etc.)(Of Þ multiplication, but it is to be done before division).
D   Division
M   Multiplication
A   Addition
S   Subtraction

Order of operations

Do operations in brackets first, strictly in the order (), {} and []
Evaluate exponents (powers, roots, etc.)
Perform division and multiplication, working from left to right. (Division and multiplication rank equally and done left to right).
Perform addition and subtraction, working from left to right. (Addition and subtraction rank equally and done left to right).

Simplification rules for real number, indices, surds, and some series

- If m is a real number, then its absolute value can   defined as
- $|m| = m$, if $m > 0$; otherwise, $-m$, if $m < 0$;
- $a^m x a^n = a^{m+n}$;
- $a^m \div a^n = a^{m-n}$;
- $(a^m)^n = a^{mn}$;
- $(ab)^n = a^n b^n$;
- $a^0 = 1$;
- $(a/b)^n = a^n/b^n$;
- $a^{-n} = 1/a^n$;

- $(\sqrt[n]{a})^n = a$;

- $\dfrac{\sqrt[n]{a}}{\sqrt[n]{b}} = \sqrt[n]{\dfrac{a}{b}}$;

- $\sqrt[m]{\sqrt[n]{a}} = \sqrt[mn]{a}$;

- $\sqrt[n]{a} * \sqrt[n]{b} = \sqrt[n]{ab}$;

- $1 + 2 + 3 + 4 + 5 + \ldots\ldots + n = \dfrac{n(n+1)}{2}$;

- $1^2 + 2^2 + 3^2 + 4^2 + 5^2 + \ldots\ldots + n^2 = \dfrac{n(n+1)(2n+1)}{6}$;

- $1^3 + 2^3 + 3^3 + 4^3 + 5^3 + \ldots\ldots + n^3 = [\dfrac{n(n+1)}{2}]^2$;

- ❖ **Common formulas to remember**
- ❖ $a^2 - b^2 = (a - b)(a + b)$
- ❖ $(a + b)^2 = a^2 + 2ab + b^2$
- ❖ $a^2 + b^2 = (a - b)^2 + 2ab$
- ❖ $(a - b)^2 = a^2 - 2ab + b^2$
- ❖ $(a + b + c)^2 = a^2 + b^2 + c^2 + 2ab + 2ac + 2bc$
- ❖ $(a + b + c)^3 = a^3 + b^3 + c^3 + 3(a + b)(b + c)(c + a)$
- ❖ $a^3 + b^3 + c^3 - 3abc = (a + b + c)(a^2 + b^2 + c^2 - ab - ac - bc)$
- ❖ $(a - b - c)^2 = a^2 + b^2 + c^2 - 2ab - 2ac + 2bc$

- ❖ $(a + b)^3 = a^3 + 3a^2b + 3ab^2 + b^3$; $(a + b)^3 = a^3 + b^3 + 3ab(a + b)$
- ❖ $(a - b)^3 = a^3 - 3a^2b + 3ab^2 - b^3$
- ❖ $a^3 - b^3 = (a - b)(a^2 + ab + b^2)$
- ❖ $a^3 + b^3 = (a + b)(a^2 - ab + b^2)$
- ❖ $(a + b)^3 = a^3 + 3a^2b + 3ab^2 + b^3$
- ❖ $(a - b)^3 = a^3 - 3a^2b + 3ab^2 - b^3$
- ❖ $(a + b)^4 = a^4 + 4a^3b + 6a^2b^2 + 4ab^3 + b^4)$
- ❖ $(a - b)^4 = a^4 - 4a^3b + 6a^2b^2 - 4ab^3 + b^4)$
- ❖ $a^4 - b^4 = (a - b)(a + b)(a^2 + b^2)$
- ❖ $a^5 - b^5 = (a - b)(a^4 + a^3b + a^2b^2 + ab^3 + b^4)$
- ❖ **If n is a natural number**, $a^n - b^n = (a - b)(a^{n-1} + a^{n-2}b + ... + b^{n-2}a + b^{n-1})$
- ❖ **If n is even** (n = 2k), $a^n + b^n = (a + b)(a^{n-1} - a^{n-2}b + ... + b^{n-2}a - b^{n-1})$
- ❖ **If n is odd** (n = 2k + 1), $a^n + b^n = (a + b)(a^{n-1} - a^{n-2}b + ... - b^{n-2}a + b^{n-1})$
- ❖ $(a + b + c + ...)^2 = a^2 + b^2 + c^2 + ... + 2(ab + ac + bc + ...$
- ❖ $(x + a)(x + b) = x^2 + (a + b)x + ab$
- ❖ $(x + a)(x - b) = x^2 + (a - b)x - ab$
- ❖ $(x - a)(x + b) = x^2 + (b - a)x - ab$
- ❖ $(x - a)(x - b) = x^2 - (a + b)x + ab$
- ❖ $(x + y + z)^2 = x^2 + y^2 + z^2 + 2xy + 2yz + 2xz$
- ❖ $(x + y - z)^2 = x^2 + y^2 + z^2 + 2xy - 2yz - 2xz$
- ❖ $(x - y + z)^2 = x^2 + y^2 + z^2 - 2xy - 2yz + 2xz$
- ❖ $(x - y - z)^2 = x^2 + y^2 + z^2 - 2xy + 2yz - 2xz$
- ❖ $x^3 + y^3 + z^3 - 3xyz = (x + y + z)(x2 + y2 + z2 - xy - yz - xz)$
- ❖ $x^2 + y^2 + z^2 - xy - yz - zx = ½ [(x-y)^2 + (y-z)^2 + (z-x)^2]$

Natural Numbers – All positive or non-negative counting numbers. The set of natural numbers are commonly denoted as N.

Example - (1, 2, 3,4.....∞).

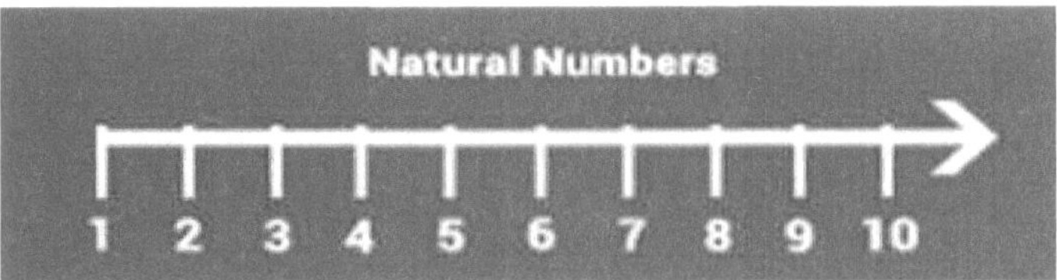

Whole Numbers – If we add zero in natural numbers set then it becomes whole numbers set.

Example - (0, 1, 2, 3,4.....∞).

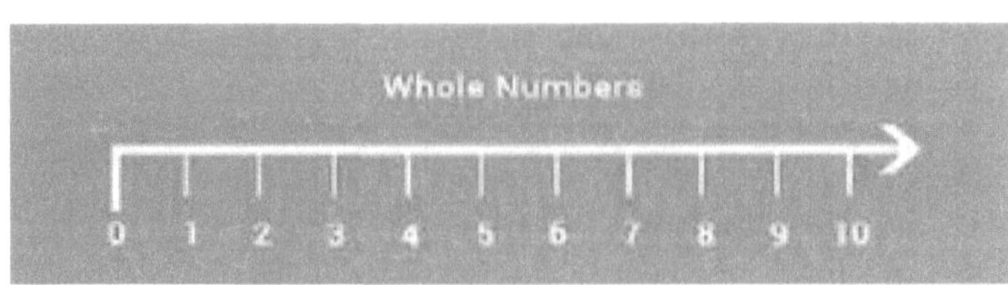

Integers – Integers are all whole numbers which include negative numbers as well as positive numbers.
Example - (∞......-4,-3,-2,-1,0,1,2,3,4,5....∞).

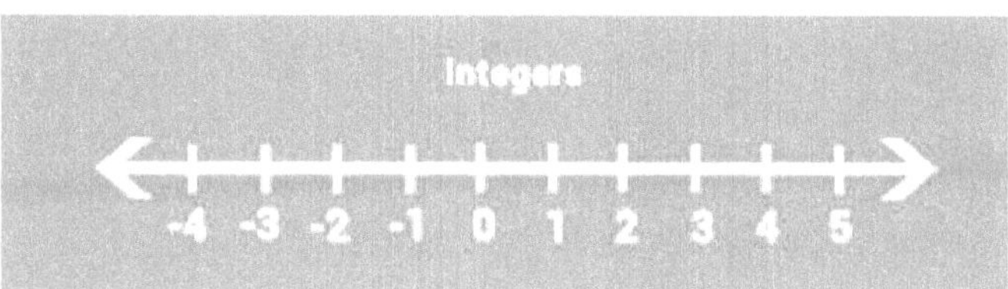

Even & Odd Numbers – If the number is divided by 2 then it is called even number and if it is not then the numbers are called odd numbers.
Example - (0,2,4,6,8,10,12.....∞) are even numbers and (1,3,5,7,9,11,13,15,17,19....∞) are odd numbers.

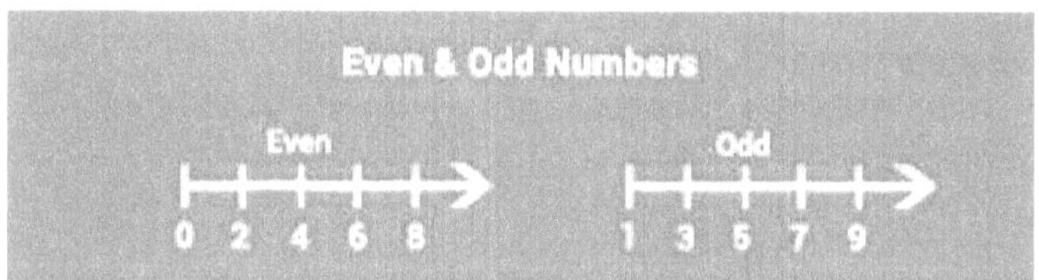

Prime Numbers – If a number is divided by itself only then it is called prime number. Prime Numbers can be positive or negative except 1.
Example - (2,3,5,7,11,13,17,19,23,29,31,37,41,43,47,53,59,61....∞)

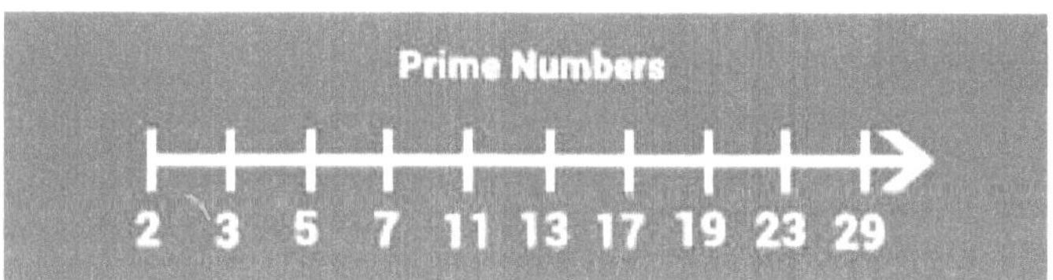

Composite Numbers – Natural numbers which are not prime are called composite numbers.
Example – (4,6,8,9,10,12,14,15,16,18,20,21,22,........... ∞)

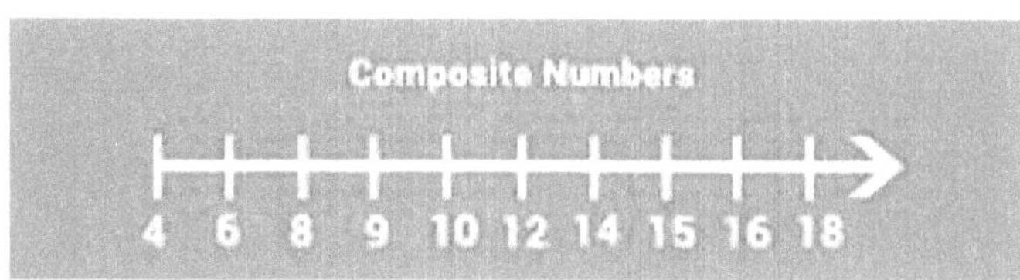

Co-Prime Numbers - Two natural number a and b are said to be co-prime if their HCF is 1.

In a simpler way, two integers (a and b) are co-prime (or relatively prime) if they share no common factors. In other words, there is no number, other than 1, that divides both a and b evenly.
Example - 6 and 35 are co-prime, because the factors of 6, 2 and 3, do not divide 35 evenly. 6 and 27 are not co-prime, because 3 divides both 6 and 27.

In case we have given with the quotient or remainder and have to find out the values of dividend or divisor, then we can use the formula given below-
*"Dividend = (Divisor * Quotient) + Remainder Or x = kq + r"*

Arithmetic Progression

If An A.P. with first term a and common difference d is given as-
a, (a+d), (a+2d), (a+3d), ... a, (a+d), (a+2d), (a+3d) ,.....
Then the formula to calculate its nth term will be – Tn = a + (n−1) * d.
The sum of n terms of this A.P.
Sn = (n2) * [2a +(n − 1) * d]Sn = (n2) ∗ (first term + last term).
Also practice with -
(1+2+3+.........+n) = ½ * n * (n+1)
(12+22+32+.........+n2) = 1/6 * n * (n+1) * (2n+1)
(13+23+33+.........+n3) = 1/4 * n2 * (n+1) * 2.

Geometric Progression
A G.P. with first term a and common ratio r is –
a, ar, ar2, ... : a, ar, ar2, ...
In this G.P. nth term = Tn = a*r$^{(n-1)}$
Sum of n terms=
Sn = a * (1−r^n) / (1−r)Sn = a * (1−r^n) / (1−r); when r>1.

Number System Formulas – Learn the Basics!

- 1 + 2 + 3 + 4 + 5 + ... + n = n(n + 1)/2
- (12 + 22 + 32 + ... + n2) = n (n + 1) (2n + 1) / 6
- (13 + 23 + 33 + ... + n3) = (n(n + 1)/ 2)2
- Sum of first n odd numbers = n2
- Sum of first n even numbers = n (n + 1)
- (a + b)*(a - b) = (a2 - b2)
- (a + b)*2 = (a2 + b2 + 2ab)
- (a - b)*2 = (a2 + b2 - 2ab)
- (a + b + c)*2 = a2 + b2 + c2 + 2(ab + bc + ca)
- (a3 + b3) = (a + b)*(a2 - ab + b2)
- (a3 - b3) = (a - b)*(a2 + ab + b2)
- (a3 + b3 + c3 - 3abc) = (a + b + c)*(a2 + b2 + c2 - ab - bc - ac)
- When a + b + c = 0, then a3 + b3 + c3 = 3abc
- (a + b)*n = an + (nC1)*an-1b + (nC2)*an-2b2 + ... + (nCn-1)*abn-1

We know that GCD $_{(a,b)}$ x LCM$_{(a,b)}$ =a x b

We know co-prime for LCM is multiplication of the two numbers & GCM will be 1.

We know that the difference between two consecutive integers is always 1.

The number 1 is neither a prime number nor a composite number.

The number 2 is the only even number which is prime.

Rules of Perfect Square:

We know that a perfect square does not end with 2, 3, 7 or 8. No perfect square ends with an odd number of zeros.

Perfect Squares can be recognised by the fact that all of their prime factors have even multiplicities.

Perfect Squares (Unit Digit – 0, 1, 4, 5, 6, 9)

Unit's Digit	0	1	4	5	6	9
Ten's Digit	0	Even	Even	2	Odd	Even

The power cycle of the digits from 0 – 9 is given below:

Last Digit	Power Cycle	Frequency
0	0	1
1	1	1
2	2,4,8,6	4
3	3,9,7,1	4
4	4,6	2
5	5	1
6	6	1
7	7,9,3,1	4
8	8,4,2,6	4
9	9,1	2

Important properties of GCM and LCM

- ❖ Product of two numbers = LCM of the numbers x HCF of the numbers
- ❖ HCF or GCD of given numbers always divides their LCM
- ❖ HCF or GCD of given fractions =GCD of Numerators / LCM of Denominator
- ❖ LCM of given fractions = LCM of Numerators / GCD of Denominator

Digit & Number ---

1. Numbers: - 1,2,3,4,5,6,7,8,9,0

2. Numbers: - 0,1,2,3…. 100 … 10000 … (All digits are numbers but not all numbers are digits). There are two types of values: a) absolute value, b) place value

3. Natural number: - 1, 2, 3 4 …

4. Whole number: - 0, 1,2,3,4…

5. Prime number: - 2,3,5,7….

6. Compound number: - 4,6,8,9….

7. The most basic number is 2

8. 2 is a prime number but it is an even number.

9. All even numbers except 2 are composite numbers.

10. Even Number-- 2, 4, 6,8,10…

11. Odd Numbers - 1,3,5,7,9,11…

12. Serial number-- 5,6,7,8,9,10

13. Integer numbers-- -1, -2, -3, 0,1,2,3

14. Positive numbers-- 1, 2, 3 … 50 … 100

15. Negative Numbers: - -1, -2, -3…

16. The number 0 is neither positive nor negative.

17. Real numbers Real numbers are mainly of two types.

18. Rational numbers: - which can be expressed in p / q form. And q = 0 is not. E.g.- 2/3, 20 $\sqrt{9}$, -8

19. Irrational numbers: - which cannot be expressed in p / q form.
20. e.g.- √2, √3

21. The main feature of real numbers is that their square values are always positive.

22. Rules of Divisibility:-

23. All numbers are divisible by 1.

24. All even numbers are divisible by 2. That is Digits 0,2,4,6 or 8 are divisible by 2. E.g., 12, 24, 36, 48 etc.

25. If the sum of the digits of a number in a corner is divisible by 3, that number is also divisible by 3. For example, the sum of the digits of the number 123 = 1 + 2 + 3 = 6. Here the number 6 is divisible by 3. So the number 123 is also divisible by 3.

26. Note: If the result is too large, then the result obtained should be left in the same formula again to see if it is divisible by 3. We have to continue like this. For example, the sum of the digits of the number 987987987 is 72. Again, the sum of the digits of the number 72 is 9. Thus the last result obtained is 9 since the number 9 is divisible by 3, so the number 987987987 is also divisible by 3.

27. If the number formed by the unit and the decimal digit of the number in the corner is divisible by 4, then the whole number is also divisible by 4. Again, even if there is 00 (two zeros) at the end of the number in the corner, that number is divisible by 4. For example, the number 12340 is the number 40, which is divisible by 4. So the number 12340 is also divisible by 4.

28. If the single local digit of a number in a corner is 0 or 5 then that number will be divisible by 5. E.g., 105, 120 etc.

29. We know 6 = 2 X 3 so if the number in the corner is divisible by 2 and 3 at the same time, then that number is divisible by 6. Simply put, even numbers that are divisible by 3 are also divisible by 6. E.g., 18,72 etc.

30. If the number formed by the last three digits of the number in the corner is divisible by 8, then that number will also be divisible by 8. Again, if there are 000 (three zeros) at the end of the number in the corner, then that number is divisible by 7.

31. For example, the number formed by the last three digits of the number 12344 is 344 since the number 344 is divisible by 8, so the number 12344 is also divisible by 8.

32. The formula for the divisibility of 9 is a lot like 3. That is, if the sum of the digits of a number in a corner is divisible by 9, that number is also divisible by 9. Details according to 3's description above. Take a look.

33. If the single local digit of a number in a corner is 0 (zero), it is divisible by 10. E.g., 30,500 etc.

34. If the sum of the even local digits of the number in the corner and the sum of the odd local digits are equal to each other, the number is divisible by 11.

35. For example, the sum of the even local digits of the number 123453 = 1 + 3 + 5 = 9 And the sum of the odd local numbers = 2 + 4 + 3 = 9. The two fruits are equal to each other. So the number 123453 is divisible by 11.

36. 12 = 2 X 2 X 3 = 4 X 3

37. So even numbers, divisible by both 3 and 4, are divisible by 12. For example, the number 540 is an even number and divisible by 3 and 4. So the number 540 is divisible by 12.

38. If the sum of the even and odd place numbers of the digits consisting of three digits to the right of the number is 0, then it is divisible by 7.
For example, 264 389 132 is the sum of the numbers of odd places consisting of three digits to the right of the number (132 + 264) = 396, the sum of the numbers of even places is 389,396-389) = 7

39. The formula for divisibility by 13 is similar to this formula.

Average and Statistics

Mean=the total sum of numbers divided by total frequencies of these numbers. (The number of times a value occurs in a set of values is its frequency)

Mode: The mode is the number with the highest frequency (when the frequency is at-least 2 or more).

Median: The median of a set of numbers is the one lying in the exact middle of the sequence.(For odd number of numbers , the middle position refers to the (number of numbers – 1) / 2.

Variance: The average of the squared differences from the Mean. Variance is the expectation of the squared deviation of a random variable from its mean.
Variance for N observations is define as : Variance $=\sum 1/N(X1\text{-Mean})^2$

Standard Deviation: The standard Deviation is a measure of how spreads out numbers are. Standard Deviation= V variance

A Standard Deviation close to 0 indicates that the data points tend to be very close to the mean of the set.
A high standard deviation indicates that the data points are spread out over a wider range of values.

Average of Mean or Arithmetic Mean (M) = sum of elements / total number of elements

Dispersion = Maximum – Minimum

Relative Dispersion = Dispersion / Mean

Average Speed = Total distance / Total time

The value of Arithmetic Mean is always in between the numbers.

We know that Arithmetic Progression >= Geometrical Progression. When all numbers are equal then AP=GP.

If two or more positive numbers whose sum is constant, then the square of numbers will be minimum when the numbers are equal.

The Average of odd numbers from 1 to n = (last odd number + 1) / 2
The average of even numbers from 1 to n = (last even number + 2) / 2

If n is odd then the average of n consecutive numbers, consecutive even numbers or consecutive odd numbers is always the middle number.

If n is even then the average of n consecutive numbers, consecutive even numbers or consecutive odd numbers is always the average of middle two numbers.

The average of first consecutive even numbers is (n+1)
The average of first n consecutive odd numbers is n.

The Geometric Mean- The geometric mean is defined as the nth root of the product of n numbers.

Geometric Mean of x1,x2,...,xn is denoted by :

$$G.M. = \sqrt[n]{X1 \times x2 \times ....\times Xn}$$

Clock Hands

> **Note:**

> In every 24 hours , hand coincide 22 number of times.(They are at 12:00 , 1:05, 2:10, 3:15, 4:20, 5:25, 6:30,7:35,8:40,9:45,10:50 in 12 hours span. The hands would not overlap at 11:55, since the hour hand is slowly moving towards 12).

> Total angle in a clock $=360^0$, there are 60 minutes , for every minutes the angle will be $360^0/60=6^0$. So, the minute hand covers 6^0 per minute.

> The hour hand covers 360^0 in 12 hours. So, hour hand covers 30^0 per hour. So, hour $(1/2)^0$ per minute.

> Thus in 1 minute, the minute hand gains $5(1/2)^0$ than the hour hand.

> The minute hand moves 12 times as fast as the hour hand.

> We know that angle between hour and minute hand will be 0^0 when they are one over the other i.e. overlap.

> When the hands are coincident, the angle between them is 0^0.

> When the hands point in opposite direction, the angle between them is 180^0.

> The angle between the two hands is 0^0 and 180^0.

> Angle between hour and minute $(\Theta)=1/2[60H-11M]$, H=hour , M = minute and At 12:00 the value of H=0.

> In a period of 12 hours, the hands make an angle of:

1) 0^0 with each other (i.e. they coincide with each other) 11 times.
2) 180^0 with each other (i.e. they lie on the same straight line) 11 times
3) 90^0 or any other angle with each other 22 times.

➢ In Every hour:
1) Both the hands coincide once.
2) The hands are in opposite direction once and hands are 30 minutes space apart.
3) The hands are twice at right angles. In this position, hands are 15 minutes spaces apart.
4) The time gap between any 2 coincidences is 12/11 hours or 65(5/11) minutes.

Permutation and Combinations Tips and Tricks and Shortcuts

Permutation is basically called as an arrangement where order does matters. Here we need to arrange the digits, numbers, alphabets, colours and letters taking some or all at a time. It is represented as ^nP_r .

Permutation : Arrangements of digits, numbers, alphabets ,colours. Letters

Clue : Arrangement , Schedule, Order

Note :

1. ^nP_r = n! / (n-r)!

2. If from the total set of n numbers p is of one kind and q, r are others respectively then ^nP_r = n! / p! × q! × r!.

3. ^nP_n = n!
4. The number of ways to arrange things
5. Order matters.
6. Number of Permutation is always greater than Number of Combination

Combination is basically called as a selection where order does not matters. Here we need to choose the digits, numbers, alphabets, colours and letters taking some or all at a time. It is represented as ^nC_r.

Here, A selection of objects in which order is not important.

Ex:- 8 people pair up to do an assignment. How many different pairs are there?

Combination: Selection of subjects, food, cloths, menu, teams

Clue: Committee, Group, Set

Note:

- ^nC_r = n!/ r! × (n-r)!
- $^nC_0$ = 1
- ^nC_n = 1
- ^nC_r = $^nC_{n-r}$
- ^nC_a = ^nC_b => a = b => a+b = n
- $^nC_0$ + $^nC_1$+ $^nC_2$+ $^nC_3$+ ....+ ^nC_n = 2^n
- The number of ways to choose things
- Order does not matter

- Number of Combination is always lesser than Number of Permutation

Permutation vs. Combination

In both the things main difference are of order .In permutation order matters while in combination it does not.
Basic Difference:
- order
- arrange or choose
- number of permutation > number of combination

1.In how many ways can the letters of the word 'LEADER' be arranged?

Count number of Occurrences
L – 1
E – 2
A – 1
D – 1
R – 1
Total Unique Occurrences – 6(as E repeated 2 times)
Direct Formula = (Unique Occurrences)!/(Each Individual Unique Occurrences)
so = 6!/(1!)(2!)(1!)(1!)(1!) = 360
<u>Type : Different ways to arrange (with repetition)</u>

Question: In how many ways can the letters of the word 'LEADER' be arranged?
Options:
a) 720
b) 360
c) 200
d) 120

Solution   Letter 'E' appears twice and all other letters 1L, 1A, 1D and 1R appears once in the word.
Required number of ways = {6!}/{2!} ={ 6 × 5 × 4 × 3 × 2 × 1}/{2 × 1} = 360

Type : Different ways to arrange (without repetition)

Question: How many different ways are there to arrange your first three classes if they are Math, English, and Hindi?

Options:

a) 4
b) 6
c) 120
d) 36

Solution

No of arrangement = 3! =3 x 2 x 1 =6

Type: Different ways to select (without repetition)

Question: How many different 4 digit numbers can be formed using the digits 2,3,4,5,6,7,8 no digit being repeated in any number
Options:

a) 720
b) 120
c) 24
d) 840

Solution: The thousand place can be filled in 7 ways, the hundredth place can be filled in 6 ways, the tens place can be filled in 5 ways, and the ones place can be filled in 5 ways.
Total ways = 7*6*5*4 = 840

Q: Out of 7 consonants and 4 vowels, how many words of 3 consonants and 2 vowels can be formed?
Number of ways of selecting (3 consonants out of 7) and (2 vowels out of 4)

$$= (^7C_3 \times {}^4C_2)$$

$$= \left(\frac{7 \times 6 \times 5}{3 \times 2 \times 1} \times \frac{4 \times 3}{2 \times 1} \right)$$

= 210.Number of groups, each having 3 consonants and 2 vowels = 210. Each group contains 5 letters.

Number of ways of arranging
5 letters among themselves = 5!
= 5 x 4 x 3 x 2 x 1
= 120.
Required number of ways = (210 x 120) = 25200.

Q: In a group of 6 boys and 4 girls, four children are to be selected. In how many different ways can they be selected such that at least one boy should be there?
We may have (1 boy and 3 girls) or (2 boys and 2 girls) or (3 boys and 1 girl) or (4 boys).
Required Number of ways:-

$$= (^6C_1 \times {}^4C_3) + (^6C_2 \times {}^4C_2) + (^6C_3 \times {}^4C_1) + (^6C_4)$$
$$= (^6C_1 \times {}^4C_1) + (^6C_2 \times {}^4C_2) + (^6C_3 \times {}^4C_1) + (^6C_2)$$
$$= (6 \times 4) + \left(\frac{6 \times 5}{2 \times 1} \times \frac{4 \times 3}{2 \times 1} \right) + \left(\frac{6 \times 5 \times 4}{3 \times 2 \times 1} \times 4 \right) + \left(\frac{6 \times 5}{2 \times 1} \right)$$
$$= (24 + 90 + 80 + 15)$$
$$= 209$$

Q.A box contains 2 white balls, 3 black balls and 4 red balls. In how many ways can 3 balls be drawn from the box, if at least one black ball is to be included in the draw?

$$\text{Required number of ways} = (^3C_1 \times {}^6C_2) + (^3C_2 \times {}^6C_1) + (^3C_3)$$
$$= \left(\frac{3 \times 6 \times 5}{2 \times 1} \right) + \left(\frac{3 \times 2}{2 \times 1} \times 6 \right) + 1$$
$$= (45 + 18 + 1) = 64.$$

Circular Combinations Problems

Q: If 6 people are going to sitting at a round table, but Sam will not sit next to Suzie, how many different ways can the group of 6 sit?
Couple of of ways of doing this:
First:
a. Total circular permutations = (6-1)! = 5! = 120.
b. Ways in which Sam and Suzie sit together = 2! * 4! = 2*24 = 48
Required ways = Total – Together = 120 – 48 = 72.
Second:
a. We have total of 6 places. Fix Suzie. Now Sam can't sit at either seat

beside her. So number of places where Sam can sit = 5-2 = 3.
For the other 4 people we can arrange them in 4! ways in 4 seats.
So total ways = 3 * 4! = 72.

Question 1.How many 3 letter words with or without meaning can be formed out of the letters of the word MONDAY when repetition of words is allowed?
Options:
A. 125
B. 216
C. 120
D. 320
Solution: 6 * 6 * 6 = 216
OR We can solve directly by formula $n^r = 6^3 = 216$
Correct option: B

Question 2. In how many ways the letters in the word TOOTH can be arranged?
Options:
A. 120
B. 40
C. 20
D. 30
Solution: $\frac{5!}{2! \times 2!}$
$= \frac{5 \times 4 \times 3 \times 2 \times 1}{2 \times 1 \times 2 \times 1}$
$= \frac{120}{4}$
$= 30$

Correct option: D

Question 3.How many three digit numbers can be formed using digits 2, 3, 4, 7, 9 so that the digits can be repeated.
Options:

A. 125
B. 360
C. 24
D. 6

Solution: Each place can be filled by any one of 5 digits

Total numbers = 5 * 5 *5 =125
OR We can solve directly by formula nr = 53 = 125

Question 1. A wooden box contains 2 grey balls, 3 pink balls and 4 green balls. Fins out in how many ways 3 balls can be drawn from the wooden box. Make sure that at least one pink ball is included in the draw?

Options:

A. 64
B. 46
C. 56
D. 65

Solution: According to the question, we have, (one pink and two non-pink balls) or (two pink and one non-pink balls) or (3 pink)
Therefore, required number of ways are $(^{3}C_{1} * {}^{6}C_{2}) + (^{3}C_{2} * {}^{6}C_{1}) + (^{3}C_{3}) = 45 +18 + 1 = 64$
Correct option: A

Question 2.There is 5 boys and 10 girls in a classroom. In how many ways teacher can select 2 boys and 3 girls to make a dance group?

Options:

A. 720
B. 1200
C. 240
D. 840
Solution: Required numbers of ways = $^{5}C_{2} * {}^{10}C_{3} = 10 * 120 = 1200$
Correct option: B

Question 3.There is 10 consonants and 5 vowels. Out of which how many words of 5 consonants and 2 vowels can be made?

Options:

A. 1270080

B. 120052

C. 210789

D. 720432

Solution: Number of ways of selecting (5 consonants out of 10) and (2 vowels out of 4) = $^{10}C_5 * {}^5C_2$ = 252

Number of ways of arranging 7 letters among themselves = 7!

=7 x 6 x 5 x 4 x3 x2 x 1

=5040

Required number of ways = (252 x 5040) = 12,70,080

Correct option: A

Probability

Note:
Probability is quantified as a number between 0 and 1, where, loosely speaking, 0 indicates impossibility and 1 indicates certainty.

The probability of an event is defined as :
P(Event)=Number of successful outcomes / Total number of possible outcomes

Outcome:
Toss a coin -> S= Head (H), Tail (T)
Toss of 2 coin simultaneously – > S= HH, HT, TH, TT
A dice thrown -> S= 1, 2, 3,4,5,6
Basket ball Game -> S= Win, Loss, Tie

1. Probability Problems on Dice

This type of Probability Questions is asked on the basis of rolling dice with six sided dots – 1, 2,3,4,5 and 6.When one dice is rolled, the number of possibilities is 6.When the two dice are rolled together, the number of possibilities is 6*6 = 36.

To check the outcomes of two dice, below we have shared the sample space of Probability.

	1	2	3	4	5	6
1	(1,1)	(1,2)	(1,3)	(1,4)	(1,5)	(1,6)
2	(2,1)	(2,2)	(2,3)	(2,4)	(2,5)	(2,6)
3	(3,1)	(3,2)	(3,3)	(3,4)	(3,5)	(3,6)
4	(4,1)	(4,2)	(4,3)	(4,4)	(4,5)	(4,6)
5	(5,1)	(5,2)	(5,3)	(5,4)	(5,5)	(5,6)

6   (6,1)   (6,2)   (6,3)   (6,4)   (6,5)   (6,6)

Here in the table, the outcomes (1,1), (2,2), (3,3), (4,4), (5,5) and (6,6) are known as doublets and the pair (1,2) and (2,1) are different outcomes.

2. Probability Problems on Coins

When we throw a coin in the air there are two conditions that can occur, whether it lands with head or with a tail.Most of the time, questions are asked on Coins problem.Probability questions on coins can be asked in three different types –

<u>When only One Coin Flipped</u> –
In this case, total events will be 2 and Probability P(E) is = 1/2.

<u>When Two Coins are Flipped</u> –
The sample space will be – {(H,T), (T,H), (H,H), (T,T)}
If the question is asked "What is the probability that both the coins shows head?", The possibility of two heads will be decided as P(H,H) = n(E)/n(S)
Putting the values in formula, we can say that the probability when both the coins show head is 1/4.

When Three Coins are Flipped –
This time the sample space will be changed as - {(H,H,H), (T,T,T), (H,H,T), (H,T,H), (T,H,H), (H,T,T), (T,H,T) ,(T ,T, H)}
Here, we see the probability that both the coins show tails will be P(E) is = 3/8.

3. Probability Problems on Cards

- Questions are also asked on the basis of a well-shuffled deck of 52 Playing Cards Probability.
- Here you can clear all the concepts to attempt the Playing Cards Probability Questions.
- The deck of 52 playing cards is divided into 4 suits of 13 cards each i.e. –
- Spades (Black Cards)

- Hearts (Red Cards)
- Diamonds (Red Cards)
- Clubs (Black Cards)

- Each suit of cards contains an ace, king, queen, jack, 10, 9,8,7,6,5,4,3, and 2.
- There are total 12 face cards (King, Queen and Jack) in a deck of playing cards.

Let's clear it with a simple example –

Question – Find the probability of a jack drawn from a deck of 52 cards?

Solution –The formula is same to get the Probability i.e. Number of Favourable Outcomes/Total Number of Possible Outcome. Here we can see that the number of favourable outcomes of 'a jack' is 4 out of 52 cards and the total number of possible outcomes is 52.So, the Probability of drawing a jack is = 4/52.

- Probability is a measure of how likely an event is to occur.
- Probability is expressed in the form of fractions.
- Favourable number of outcomes
- Total number of outcomes
- Probability ranges between 0 and 1.

$$\text{Probability} = \frac{\text{Favorable number of outcomes}}{\text{Total number of outcomes}}$$

E.g. when the probability of an event is $\frac{2}{5}$

That means in a total of 5 occurrences, 2 times the occurrences are in my favour.

Favourable outcome is nothing but the condition provided to us in the question.

Example - Consider tossing a fair coin once. What is the probability of getting a heads?

Solution – The first thing is to find the values to keep in the formula. A total number of outcomes = when you toss a coin once, the possibility is that you may get tails or a heads that give us total 2 possibilities. The favourable number of outcomes = the condition given to us is to get a heads which are 1 number of time.

Right!!

Now let us put the values in the formula

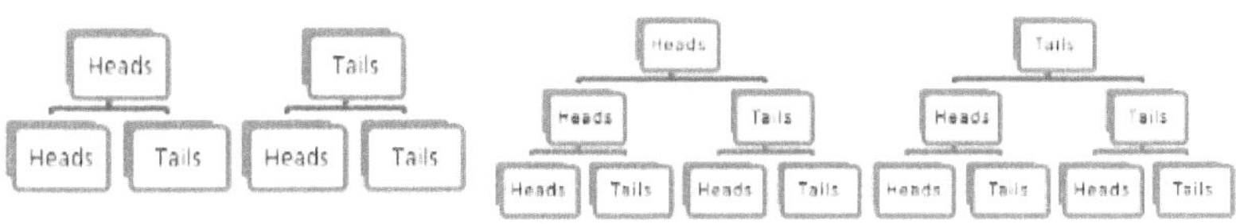

Let's talk about Dices.

A standard dice has 6 numbers on 6 faces ranging from 1 to 6.

Now if I want to determine the probability of the event of obtaining a number 4 in one roll of a dice.

The total number of outcomes = when you roll a dice once, the possibility is that you may get a number 1 or 2 or 3 or 4 or 5 or 6, which gives us a total number of 6 possibilities.

The favourable number of outcomes = the condition given to us is to get a number 4 which is 1 number of time.

$$\text{Probability} = \frac{\text{Favorable number of outcomes}}{\text{Total number of outcomes}} = \frac{1}{6}$$

Wasn't this a cake walk?

For two rolls of dice, the possibilities are as:

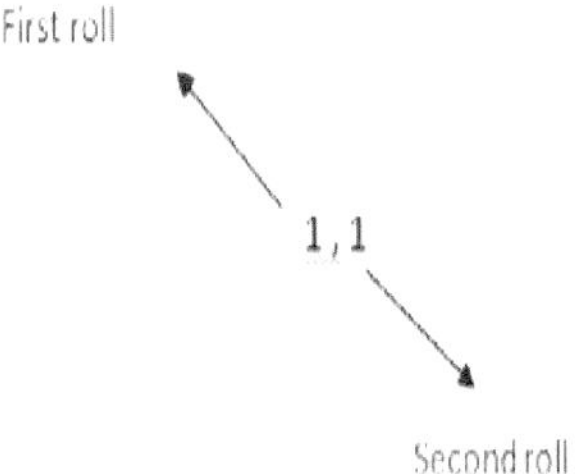

1,1	1,2	1,3	1,4		1,5	1,6
2,1	2,2	2,3	2,4		2,5	2,6
3,1	3,2	3,3	3,4		3,5	3,6
4,1	4,2	4,3	4,4		4,5	4,6
5,1	5,2	5,3	5,4		5,5	5,6
6,1	6,2	6,3	6,4		6,5	6,6

Example - Consider rolling a standard dice twice. What is the probability of getting a prime number in the first roll?

Solution – The first thing that we do is find the total number of possibilities. In the question, we need to roll the dice twice. From the above table, we get the total number of 36 possibilities. To find the favourable number of outcomes; we read the condition which is to get a prime number in the first roll. Among the numbers 1, 2, 3, 4, 5, 6 on the dice, the prime numbers are 2, 3 and 5.With these numbers on the first roll we have

2,1	2,2	2,3	2,4	2,5	2,6
3,1	3,2	3,3	3,4	3,5	3,6
5,1	5,2	5,3	5,4	5,5	5,6

these many possibilities. Total 18 Keeping the values in the formula

$$\text{Probability} = \frac{\text{Favorable number of outcomes}}{\text{Total number of outcomes}} = \frac{18}{36} = \frac{1}{2}$$

For the sum related questions on two rolls of a dice, try and remember this technique

2	12	1
3	11	2
4	10	3
5	9	4
6	8	5
7		6

For the sum related questions on two rolls of a dice, try and remember this technique.

Now, what does this mean?

The lowest sum after the two rolls of a dice is 2 from (1, 1) while the highest sum is 12 from (6, 6), which means the total number of possibilities of getting a sum of 2 or 12 is 1 (which is the number on their right most side).
Similarly, the number of possibilities of getting a sum of 3 or 11 is 2 (which is the number on their right most side) and so on.
Just a look at the above diagram will make the sum related problems of a dice easy for you.

Example – What is the probability of getting a sum 9 from two rolls of a dice?

Solution – The first thing that we do is find the total number of possibilities which is 36.

Now to get a sum of 9, from the above table, the number on the rightmost side of the row having number 9 is 4. This means 4 is the favourable number of outcomes.

Cross-check – To get sum 9, the possibilities are (4,5), (5,4), (3,6), (6,3), 4 in total, thus justifying the authenticity of the table.

Now, Putting values in the formula

$$\text{Probability} = \frac{\text{Favorable number of outcomes}}{\text{Total number of outcomes}} = \frac{4}{36} = \frac{1}{9}$$

Few practice problems:

1.   Two dice are tossed. The probability that a total score is a prime number is?

2.   Two dice are thrown simultaneously. What is the probability of getting two numbers whose product is even?

3.   In a simultaneous throw of a pair of dice, find the probability of getting equal numbers.

Another important set of question in probability consists of cards. The hierarchy below represents the types of cards in a deck.

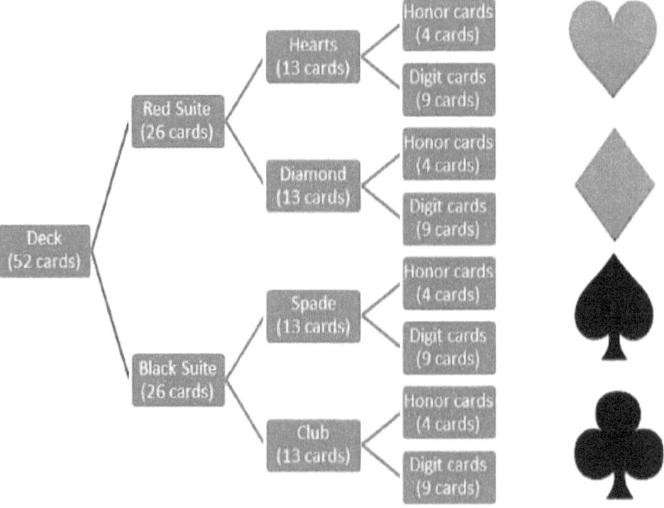

Digit cards – 2 to 10 (total 9 cards of one type and there are 4 types of cards, which gives us a total of 9 x 4 = 36 digit cards in a deck)
Honor cards – Ace, King, Queen, Jack (4 of each type and there are 4 types, which gives us a total of 4 x 4 = 16 honor cards in a deck)
When we talk about the favorable condition (given to us in the question) in the problems related to cards, we need to have our concepts crystal

clear of COMBINATIONS.

Let's work with examples

Example – What is the probability of picking up an ace in a deck of 52 cards?

Solution – Now, there are 4 aces in a deck. So, the favorable condition is to pick an ace card from the 4 ace ones i.e. $^4C_1$.

To get the total number of conditions, we can pick a card from the entire deck, which gives us $^{52}C_1$.

Keeping these values in the formula gives us

$$\text{Probability} = \frac{^4C_1}{^{52}C_1} = \frac{4}{52} = \frac{1}{13}$$

Hope the concept is clear by now. How about we solve a question together?

Question - From a pack of 52 cards, two cards are drawn together at random. What is the probability of both the cards being kings?

Solution –

$$\text{Probability} = \frac{^4C_2}{^{52}C_2} = \frac{4 \times 3 / 2 \times 1}{52 \times 51 / 2 \times 1} = \frac{1}{221}$$

Question – What is the probability of drawing a card from a deck which is either a king or a Diamond card?

Solution –

$$\text{Probability} - \quad \frac{^4C_1 + {}^{12}C_1}{^{52}C_1} \quad = \quad \frac{4 + 12 = 16}{52} \quad = \quad \frac{4}{13}$$

You might be wondering about the $^{12}C_1$ as Diamond cards are total 13 in number. Well guys, when we selected a king card, which are 4 in number, the set of 4 also had a diamond card in it, Thus leaving 12 diamond cards for us to select from.
We can also select a diamond card first and then a king card. The equation then would look like

$$\frac{^{13}C_1 + {}^3C_1}{^{52}C_1}$$

The answer in both the cases will be similar.
Few practice problems:

1. Two cards are drawn together from a pack of 52 cards. The probability that one is a spade and one is a heart, is.

2. One card is drawn at random from a pack of 52 cards. What is the probability that the card drawn is an Honor card (Jack, Queen, and King only)?
3. If three cards are drawn at random from a well shuffled deck. What is the probability of picking out 2 Jacks of red color and 1 black-color digit card?
4. 2 cards are drawn at random from a deck. Find the probabilities of picking out

- o Exactly 2 Queens.
- o At least one Queen.
- o No Queen.
- o At most 1 Queen.

Last (but not the least) are the questions asking you the probabilities with the condition when a ball is picked from a bag.
Let's start the concept with an example.

Example – What is the probability of picking out one white ball from a bag that has 4 white balls in it?
Solution – The bag contains white and white balls only. So no matter how many times you take out a ball it is going to be white undoubtedly. Therefore, the probability of the event happening becomes 1.

Another Example,

Example – What is the probability of picking out a blue ball from a bag that contains 7 black balls?
Solution –I hope the answer's pretty easy. 0 (Isn't it!)

Example – A bag contains 6 Blue, 4 White balls. If 2 balls are drawn at a time, find the probability of picking out balls of different colors.
Solution –As there are 2 colors and 2 balls are drawn then one of them must be blue while the other one must be white. (Clear!)

Therefore

$$\text{Probability} = \frac{^6C_1 \times {}^4C_1}{^{10}C_2} = \frac{6 \times 4 = 24}{10 \times 9 / 2 \times 1} = \frac{8}{15}$$

What if in the same question, the condition is changed to "If 2 balls are drawn at a time, find the probability of picking out balls of same colour."

Then, as there are 2 colours and 2 balls are drawn then both the balls drawn are either white in colour or blue in colour. (Clear!). Therefore, the equation changes as follows

$$\text{Probability} = \frac{^6C_2 + {}^4C_2}{^{10}C_2} = \frac{6 \times 5 / 2 \times 1 + 4 \times 3 / 2 \times 1}{10 \times 9 / 2 \times 1} = \frac{7}{15}$$

✓ Whenever the condition comprises of the word "Either…Or", the arithmetic sign is Addition (+).
✓ Whenever the condition comprises of the word "And", the arithmetic sign is Multiplication (x).

Let us discuss one other example.

Example – A bag contains 5 White, 2 Red, 3 Black balls. If 2 balls are drawn at a time, find the probability of picking out at least one white ball.

Solution – The word "at least" implies the picking of either 1 white ball or both white balls. Now, if there is 1 white ball in the selection that means other one picked ball is of other color (meaning red and black in this case). And 2 white balls means there cannot be any other colour ball.

Therefore, the equation becomes

$$\text{Probability} - \frac{(^5C_1 \times {}^5C_1) + {}^5C_2}{^{10}C_2} - \frac{(5 \times 5) + 10 - 35}{10 \times 9 / 2 \times 1 - 45} - \frac{7}{9}$$

Trick – What if rather than calculating all the possibilities of at least (minimum 1 ball), I simply consider the possibility of no white balls and subtracted it from 1(highest probability of an event happening)

If there is no white ball, this means all the two balls are selected from 2 red and 3 black balls, means total of 5 balls.

Selecting 2 balls from 5 gives me $^5C_2$.
And the total number of possibilities is selecting two balls from total number of balls (in this case 10 balls), which is $^{10}C_2$.

So, the probability becomes

$$\frac{^5C_2}{^{10}C_2}$$

The calculation of which gives me

$$\frac{2}{9}$$

Now, don't forget the step where we promised to subtract it from highest probability 1.

So,

$$1 - \frac{2}{9}$$

gives me

$$\frac{7}{9}$$

This is the final probability.

Isn't it the same to what we calculated earlier? The trick takes some time but with some practice, you will get a hang of it. The trick with "at least" can be applied to the problems with deck of cards too.

PROFIT, LOSS & DISCOUNT

- ❖ Let P be the principal amount and R be the rate of interest, then after n years, we have
  P $(1+R/100)^n$ as principal with interest if interest compounded yearly.
- ❖ The % loss ={(CP-SP) / CP} 100
- ❖ Profit= S.P – C.P
- ❖ Profit% = {(S.P – C.P)/C.P}*100 = (Profit/C.P)* 100
- ❖ Loss = C.P – S.P
- ❖ Loss% = {(C.P – S.P)/C.P}*100 = (Loss/C.P)*100
- ❖ S.P = (100 + PROFIT% / 100)*C.P   OR   S.P = (100 – LOSS% / 100)*C.P
- ❖ C.P = {100 /(100 + PROFIT%)}*S.P   OR   C.P = {100 /(100 - LOSS%)}*S.P
- ❖ SUCCESSIVE DISCOUNTS:

- ❖ Certain discount id given on an item whose Marked Price is MP. If further discounts are given on this discounted price, such discounts are referred to as Successive Discount. If the Successive Discount are a%, b%, and C% on an item whose

40

selling price is SP, then the effective price after all the discounts are as below:

- SP = MP x {(100-a)(100-b)(100-c)} / (100 x 100 x 100)

Points should be remember-

- Discount = M.P – S.P
- Discount% = (Discount / M.P) * 100
- S.P = M.P{(100 - Discount%) / 100}
- M.P = {(100*S.P) / (100 – Discount %)}

YEAR, WEEK & DAY

❖ Sunday-0 day, Monday-1st day, Tuesday- 2nd day,…..,Saturday-6th day. For 0 odd days, the day will be Sunday; for 1 odd day, the day will be Monday; for 2 odd days, it will be Tuesday; for 3 odd days, it will be Wednesday and so on.

❖ In an ordinary year, there are 365 days, which means 52 x 7 + 1, or 52 weeks and one day. This additional day is called an odd day. The concept of odd days is very important in calendars.

❖ In a century - i.e. 100 years, there will be 24 leap years and 76 non-leap years. This means that there will be 24 x 2 + 76 x 1 = 124 odd days. Since, 7 odd days make a week, to find out the net odd days, divide 124 by 7. The remainder is 5. This is the number of odd days in a century.

❖ Odd days: The days more than the complete number of weeks in given period are called odd days. In any year, there are 52 complete weeks.

❖ Ordinary Year: An ordinary year has 365 days i.e. 52 weeks and 1 odd day.

❖ Leap Year: It should be divisible by 4 (Every 4th century is a leap year and no other century is a leap year.) We know that for a year to be leap year, there are two conditions: i) it should be divisible by 4 ii) If it is divisible by 100, it should also be divisible by 400. For better understanding, we may take example of four consecutive years 1899,1900,1901,1902 in which no leap year occurs. By condition i), 1899, 1901, 1902 are non-leap years. Again by the condition ii), 1900 is also a non-leap year.

❖ A leap year has 366 days i.e. 52 weeks and 2 odd days. A non-leap year have 1 odd day(365/7=52 weeks 1day)

❖ 100 Years = 76 ordinary years + 24 leap years = (76 x 1 + 24 x 2) odd days = 124 odd days = (17 weeks + 5 days) = 5 odd days.

You should memorize the Following-

• Number of odd days in 100 years = 5

• Number of odd days in 200 years = (5 x 2) (mod 7) = 3 odd day
• Number of odd days in 300 years = (5 x 3) (mod 7) = 1 odd day

• Number of odd days in 400 years = (5 x 4 + 1) (mod 7) = 0 odd day (Since, year 400 is a leap year; it has 1 extra odd day than ordinary year.

• Similarly, each one of 800 years, 1200 years, 1600 years, 2000 years etc. has 0 odd days.

• Two months will have same calendar (the same days and dates), if number of odd days between them are 0 (i.e. multiple of 7).

- The day after tomorrow is Friday. Then today is Wednesday. Yesterday was Tuesday. Day before yesterday was Monday. Day before the day before yesterday was Sunday.

Important Tips:

- ❖ The last day of a century must be Sunday, Monday, Wednesday or Friday.
- ❖ An ordinary year always begins and ends on the same day of the week.
- ❖ Number of odd days of 1900 years = 1 odd day.

<u>Making Equation to solve</u>

- ❖ If two conditions are given then only we can use two variables because to find the values of two variables we require at least two equations.

- ❖ Express the situation in terms of the above variables.

- ❖ Solve the equation to find the value of the variables.

- ❖ In case of two variable equations, try to equate the two equations by applying multiplication or division.

Problem & Solve by making equation

1. Suppose $a^2 + b^2 = 4(a+3b-10)$, where a and b are two real numbers. Then which of the following is true? (CSIR-NET-NOV-2020)

    a) a> b   **b) a< b**   c) a = b   d) from the above equation nothing can be said about the relationship between a and b.

Hint:

$a^2 + b^2 = 4(a+3b-10)$ or, $a^2 + b^2 = 4a + 12b - 40$ or, $a^2 + b^2 - 4a - 12b + 40 = 0$

or, $a^2 - 4a + 4 + b^2 - 12b + 36 = 0$ or, $(a - 2)^2 + (b - 6)^2 = 0$. Therefore, we may say that $(a - 2)^2 = 0$, $(b - 6)^2 = 0$

or, $a - 2 = 0$, $b - 6 = 0$ or, a=2, b = 6 i.e. a<b

2. In a class, there is one 1 pencil for every two students, one eraser for three student, and one ruler for every four students. If the total number of these stationery items required is 65. How many students are present in the class? (CSIR-NET-NOV-2020)

    a) 55   **b) 60**   c) 65   d) 70

Hint:
Let us assume that the students present in the class are X. Therefore,
The total number of stationery will be
X/2 +X/3 +X/4 = (6X+4x+3X) / 12 = 13X/12. As per question, 13X/12=65
or 13X = 65*12 or, X=65*12/13 =60.

3. The present age of a father is square of the age of his son. After six years, the age of the father would be 3($^1/_2$) times the age of the son. The present age of the father is? (CSIR-NET-NOV-2020)

    a) 36   b) 42   c) 48   d) 54

Hint:

Let us assume the present age of the son is x. So, the present age of the father will be x^2. After six years the age of the father would be 3($^1/_2$) times the age of the son i.e. x^2 + 6 = 3($^1/_2$)(x+6) or, x^2 + 6 =$^7/_2$(x+6)
Or, 2 x^2+12=7x+42 or, 2 x^2 -7x -30 =0 or, 2 x^2 -12x +5x -30=0 or, 2x(x-6) + 5(x-6) =0 or,(x-6)(2x+5)=0, therefore,
x=6 or x=5/2=2.5. If x=6 then x^2 =36 and x+6=12 and x^2+6=42 and 42/12=3($^1/_2$). If x=2.5 then x^2=6.25 and x+6=8.5, similarly x^2+6=12.25 and 12.25/8.5=1.44which is not equal to 3.5. So the present age of the father will be 36 years.

4. Of the employees of a company 60 are male and the rest are female. The overall average salary is Rs.9000; the average for the female employees is Rs.12000 and that of male employees is Rs.7000. The difference between the numbers of male and female employees is? (CSIR-NET-NOV-2020)

    a) 30   b) 10   c) 20   d) 40

Hint:

Suppose X is the number of female employees. Therefore, total employees = x + 60, Now the total salary of all employees = 9000(x+60). The salary of x number of females = 12000x and the salary of 60 men

employees = 60*7000=420000. Now as per given condition, 9000(x+60)= 12000x+420000
or, 9000x+540000= 12000x +420000 or, 12000x-9000x= 540000-420000
or, 3000x= 120000 or, x=120000/3000 =40. So, the difference between the male and female employee = 60-40=20

5. An expenditure of Rs.96 was supposed to be shared equally by all the students in a class. Since four students did not contribute, the remaining students had to contribute an additional amount of Rs. 4 each. How many students contributed? (CSIR-NET-NOV-2020).

a) 8   b) 12   c) 16   d) 24

Hint:

Let us assume that the number of students in the class =x , Therefore, the per student expenditure will be 96/x. Since 4 students did not contribute, i.e. x-4 students contributed then the per student expenditure will be (96/x)+4. Now as per question, {(96/x)+4}*(x-4) = 96
or, 96+4x-96*4/x-16=96 Or, $4x^2$-96*4-16x=0
Or, x^2-96=4x or x2-4x-96=0 or x^2-12x+8x-96 =0 or, x(x-12) +8(x-12)=0 or, (x-12)(x-8)=0,or x=12. So the number of students contributed = 12-4 = 8

6. In a college admission where applicants have to choose only one subject. 1/4th of the applicants opted for Biology, 1/6th for Chemistry, 1/8th for Physics and 1/12th for Maths. 18 applicants did not opt for any of the above four subjects. How many applicants were there? (CSIR-NET-NOV-2020).

a) 22   b) 24   c) 36   **d) 48**

Hint:
Let us assume that there are x number of applicants. Therefore, as per question, x −(x/4 +x/6+x/8+x/12)=18
Or, x − (6x+4x+3x+2x)/24=18 or, x-15x/24 = 18   or, 24x − 15x =18*24
or,9x=18*24 or, x=48

7. A two digit number is such that if the digit 4 is placed to its right, the value would increase by 490.Find the original number. (CSIR-NET-DEC-2019)

a) 48   **b) 54**   c) 64   d) 56

Hint:

a) 484 - 48 $\neq$490   b) 544 $-$ 54 = 490   c) 644 -64 = 580$\neq$490   d) 566 $-$ 56 = 510 $\neq$490. So the correct answer is b).

8. Some fisherman caught some fish. No one caught more than 20 fish.a1 number of fisherman caught at least one fish among them, a2 number of fisherman caught at least two fishes among them , and so on and a20 number of fisherman caught exactly 20fish among them. How many fish were caught?(CSIR-NET-JUN-2017)

   a) **$a_1+a_2+a_3+...+a_{20}$**   b) $a_1+2a_2+3a_3+...+20a_{20}$ c) $20(a_1+a_2+a_3+...+a_{20})$
   d)$20(a_1+2a_2+3a_3+...+20a_{20})$

Hint:
As a_1 number of fisherman caught at least 1 fish, so the total fish caught
= $(a_1-a_2).1$
Similarly a_2 number of fisherman caught at least 2 fish, so, the total fish caught = $(a2-a3).2$
Similarly a_3 number of fisherman caught at least 3 fish, so, the total fish caught = $(a3-a4).3$
Similarly a_{20} number of fisherman caught 20 fish, so, the total fish caught =$a_{20}.20$
Summing up the terms $(a_1-a_2).1+ (a_2-a_3).2+(a_3-a_4).3+..........+ a_{20}.20$ = $a_1-a_2+2a_2-2a_3+3a_3-3a_4+...-a_{20}.19+a_{20}.20$
= $a_1+a_2+a_3+3a_4+...+a_{20}.$

9. If NET14 and NET15 are 5 digits numbers such that their sum =157229, then N+E+T would be?(CSIR-NET-DEC-2017)

a) 15   **b) 21**   c) 25   d) 72

Hint: -   N E T **1 4**

```
+    N E T 1 5
     -----------------
     1572 2 9
```

As 14 +15 =29, which have a perfect match in above addition ,so rest of the figure 1572 will be equal to NET+NET=2NET.

Therefore, 2NET=1572 and NET= 786 ,which means N=7 ,E=8 ,T= 6 , So N+E+T = 7+8+6=21 , So, answer is **b)21**.

10. A shopkeeper sells a file and a notebook for Rs.27 to the first customer, a notebook and a pen for Rs.31 to the second customer and a pen and file for Rs.29 to the third customer. The prices of the items are rounded in rupees. Which of the following inferences is correct? (CSIR-NET-JUN-2017)

a) The pen is costliest of the three.
b) The file is the costliest of the three.
c) The notebook is the costliest of the three.
d) The shopkeeper sold the different items to different customers at different rate.

Hint:

File + Notebook= 27..... (i)   Notebook + Pen = 31..... (ii)   Pen + File =29..... (iii)
Now doing (i) – (ii), we get, File +Notebook –Notebook-Pen=27-31 or, File-Pen =-4..... (iv)
Now doing (iii) + (iv), we get, Pen + File +File-Pen=29 - 4 or, 2.File=25, or, File=25/2=12.5 =13
Now, we get from (i) Notebook=27-file=27-13=14 and also get from (ii) Pen=31 – Notebook =31-14=17.

File= 13, Notebook=14, Pen=17—So, Pen is costlier of the three.

11. If 42-> 26, 71->78, 33->16, then 62->? (CSIR-NET-JUN-2017)

a)   68   b) 54   **c) 38**   d) 38

Hint:

42->26 (4/2=2 which is 1st digit of 26 and 4+2=6 which is 2nd digit of 26)
71->78 (7/1=7 which is 1st digit of 78 and 7+1=8 which is 2nd digit of 78)
33->16 (3/3=1 which is 1st digit of 16 and 3+3=6 which is 2nd digit of 16)
62->   (6/2=3 which is 1st digit and 6+2=8 which is 2nd digit i.e. the number will be 38)

12. A river is 4.1 km wide. A bridge built across it has 1/7 of its length on one bank and 1/8 of its length on the other bank. What is the total length of the bridge? (CSIR-NET-DEC-2016).

   a) 5.1 km   b) 4.9 km   **c) 5.6 km**   d) 5.4 km

Hint:
Let us assume the length of the bridge is x km. Therefore, as per question, x= x / 7+ x / 8+ 4.1
Or, x − x/7 − x/8 = 4.1 or, (56x-8x-7x) / 56 = 4.1   or, 41x = 4.1*56 or, x = 41*56/41*10 =5.6

13. Intravenous (IV) fluid to be administered to a child of 12 kg with dehydration, at a dose of 20 mg of fluid per kg of body weight, in 1 hour. What should be the drip rate (in drops/min) of IV fluid?(1 mg = 20drops) (CSIR-NET-DEC-2016)

   a) 7   **b) 80**   c) 120   d) 4

Hint:
The required dose is 20 mg of fluid per kg of body weight in 1 hour, So, for a child of 12 kg, the dose will be 12*20 =240 mg in 1 hour. So in 60 minutes it requires 240mg i.e, 240*20=4800 drops. So, in 1 minute it requires 4800/60=80 drops.

14. The sum of digits of a two-digit number is 9. If the fraction formed by taking 9 less than the number as numerator and 9 more than the number as denominator is ¾, what is the number? (CSIR-NET-DEC-2016)

a) 36   b) 63   c) 45   d) 54

Explanations:

If the number is N then N-9/N+9 = ¾ ; 4N -36 = 3N+27 ; N= 36+27=63

15. The difference between the squares of the ages (in complete years) of a father and his son is 899. The age of the father when his son was born?(CSIR-NET-JUN-2016)

   a)   Cannot be ascertained due to inadequate data
   b)   Is 27 years
   c)   Is 29 years
   d)   Is 31 years

Hint:

To solve this type of question we have to take the help of hit and trial method. Let us assume that at the time of birth of son, father is of 29 years. After 1 year father will be 30 years and son= 1 year. As per question, the difference between the squares of the ages (in complete years) of a father and his son is 899. Therefore, $30^2 - 1^2$ =899.

16. When a polynomial f(x) is divided by x – 5 or x – 3 or x – 2, it leaves a reminder of 1. Which of the following would be the polynomial? (CSIR-NET-JUN-2016)

   a) $X^3 - 10x^2 + 31x + 31$ **b) $X^3 - 10x^2 + 31x -29$**   c) $X^3 - 10x^2 + 31x - 31$ d) $X^3 - 10x^2 + 31x + 29$

Hint:

Now, we put x= 5, 3, 2 in each polynomial as per reminder theorem. Only polynomial $X^3 - 10x^2 + 31x -29$ gives reminder 1 for each.

17. How many digits are there in 3^{16} when it is expressed in the decimal form? (CSIR-NET-DEC-2015)

a) Three   b) Six   c) Seven   **d) Eight**

Hint:

$3^{16} = (3^4)^4 = (81)^4 \rightarrow (80)^4 = 8^4 \times 10^4 = 64 \times 64 \times 10^4 \rightarrow 60 \times 60 \times 10^4$, 60 x 60=3600have 4 digit and 10^4 have 4 digit, So there is total 8 digit.

18. If D + I + M = 1501
     C + I + V + I + L = 157
     L + I + V + I + D = 557
     C + I + V + I + C = 207
What is V + I + M =? (CSIR-NET-DEC-2015)

   A) Cannot be found   b) 1009   **c) 1006**   d) 509

Hint:

Here are six unknown variables, So we are using Roman number system as: I=1, V=5, L=50, C=100, D= 500, M=1000. If we put these values in above equation, we see that all the equation satisfying.
D + I + M = 500+1+1000=1501, C+I+V+I+L=100+1+5+1+50=157, L+I+V+I+D = 50+1+5+1+500=557
C+I+V+I+C= 100+1+5+1+100=207. Therefore, V+I+M= 5+1+1000=1006

19. 20% of students of a particular course get jobs within one year of passing. 20% of the remaining students get jobs by the end of second year of passing. If 16 students are still jobless, how many students had passed the course? (CSIR-NET-DEC-2014)

   a)   32   b) 64   **c) 25**   d|) 100

Hint:

Let us assume x number of students passed the Course. As 20% student get job in 1st year, so x*20/100=x/5 students get job in 1st year. The remaining student will be x-x/5=4x/5. In second year 20% of remaining students get jobs, i.e. (4x/5)(20/100)=4x/25. As per question, we may write, x −(x/5 + 4x/25) = 16 or, x-(9x/25)=16 or, 25x-9x=16*25 Or, 16x=16*25 or x=16*25/16=25

20. Three years ago, the difference in the ages of two brothers was 2 years. The sum of their present age will double in 10 years. What is the present age of the elder brother?(CSIR-NET-JUN-2014)

   a) 6   **b) 11**   c) 7   d) 9

Hint:

Let us assume that the present age of the elder brother= x and younger brother=y. Therefore the sum of their present age will be x+y and as per question (x+10)+(y+10) = 2(x+y) or x+y+20=2x+2y or, x+y=20-----(i)
Again as per question (x-3)-(y-3)=2 or. X-y=2------- (ii). Doing (i) + (ii) , we get 2x=22 or x=11. So the present age of the elder brother is 11 years.

21. Three fisherman caught fishes and went to sleep. One of them woke up, took away one fish and $1/3^{rd}$ of the remainder as his share, without other's knowledge. Later, the three of them divided the remainder equally. How many fishes were caught?(CSIR-NET-DEC-2013)

a)   58   **b) 19**   c) 76   d) 88

Hint:

Let us assume that x number of fishes were caught. One of them at night took away 1fish and then $1/3^{rd}$ of reminder fish which will be (x-1)*1/3. Rest of the fish will be (x-1)*2/3. As the fisherman divided (x-1)*2/3 fishes among 3 fisherman, this value should be multiple of 3 i.e. (x-1)*2/3 =3k, here k is an integer. Now , from option a) , we get , (58-1)*2/3=57*2/3=38 which is not the multiple of 3, Again in option b) , we get,
(19-1)*2/3=18*2/3=12 =3*4, So total 19 fishes was caught by the fisherman.

22. In an enclosure there were both crows and cows. If there are 30 heads and 100 legs, what fraction of them are crows?(CSIR-NET-DEC-2013)

a)   **1:3**   b) 1:4   c) 1:10   d) 3:10

Hint:

Let us assume that there were x crows and y cows in the enclosure. As per question, we get x+y=30 and
2x+4y=100 i.e. x+2y=50. By subtracting x+2y=50 and x+y=30 we get y=20, So x=30-21=10. There is 10 numbers of crows. Required fraction = 10/(10+20)=10/30=1/3=1:3

23. In a room, we have one grandfather, two father, two sons and a grandson. The age of one father is seven times the age of his son. The age of the other father is twice his son's age. Assuming that there are only 3 people in the room and the grandfather is 70 years old, how old is the grandson?(CSIR-NET-DEC-2013)

a) 1　　　　b) 2　　　　**c) 5**　　　　d) cannot be determined

Hint:

As there are total three persons so, we may consider this situation as A->B-> C. Here A is father of B and B is also father of C. Two father are A and B, Two sons are B and C. Grandfather is A and Grandson is C. Let us assume the age of C is x. Now the age of B will be 7x and age of A will be 14x.Now 14x=70, or, x=70/14=5.

24. A king ordered that a golden crown be made for him from 8 kg of gold and 2 kg of silver. The goldsmith took away some amount of gold and replaced it by an equal amount of silver and the crown when made, weighted 10kg. Archimedes knew that under water gold lost $1/20^{th}$ of its weight, while silver lost $1/10^{th}$. When the crown was weighted under water, it was 9.25kg. How much gold was stolen by the goldsmith?(CSIR-NET-JUN-2013)

a) 0.5 kg　　　　b) 1 kg　　　　c) 2 kg　　　　**d) 3 kg**

Hint.
Let us assume that the goldsmith stolen x kg of gold. So the gold will be (8 − x) kg. The same weight of silver was replaced. So the silver will be (2 + x)kg. Under water weight, gold lost $1/20^{th}$ and silver lost $1/10^{th}$. So under water, loss of weight can be equated as, (8-x)*1/20 + (2+x)*1/10 =10-9.25=.75 or, (8-x+4+2x)/20=0.75 or, x+12=0.75*20 or, x= 15-12=3. Gold stolen by Goldsmith =3 5kg

CLOCK HANDS

1.The number of times the minute hand and the hour hand, in a clock, are exactly above each other (i.e. angle between them is zero) from 1 am of a day to 1 am on the next day is ? (CSIR-NET-)

a) 21　　　　**b) 22**　　　　c) 23　　　　d) 24

Hint:

In every 24 hours , hand coincide 22 number of times.(They are at 12:00 , 1:05, 2:10, 3:15, 4:20, 5:25, 6:30,7:35,8:40,9:45,10:50 in 12 hours span. The hands would not overlap at 11:55, since the hour hand is slowly moving towards 12).

2. A clock takes 7 seconds to announce 7 o'clock by chiming seven times. How many seconds will this clock take to announce 10 o'clock by chiming 10 times? (CSIR-NET-NOV-2020)

a) 10　　　　b) 9.5　　　　c) 10.5　　　　d) 11

Hint: The clock takes 7 seconds to chiming 7 times , so , it takes 1 second to chiming 1 time and therefore it takes 10 seconds to chiming 10 times.

3. Clock A loses 4 minutes every hour, clock B always shows the correct time and clock C gains 3 minutes every hour. On a Monday, all the three clocks showed the same time 8 pm. On the following Wednesday, when the clock C shows 2 pm, what time will clock A show? (CSIR-NET-DEC-2019)

a) 7:20 am   b) 8:40 am   **c) 9:20 am**   d) 10:40 am

Hint:

Hour	C-Fast 3 minutes/hr	B-right time	A slow 4 minute/hr
8 pm-Monday->	Right time	Right time	Right time
Wednesday ->	2 pm -> 42hr-> 42*3=126minutes slow Now the right time-> 2 p.m -2 hr 6 min=11:54am	Right time – 11:54 am - >12 noon	12 noon-> 40*4 minute fast-> 160 minute->2 hr 40 minutes fast-> 12 noon – 2:40 -> 9:20 am

4. How many times starting at 1:00 pm would the minute and hour hands of a clock make an angle of 40^0 with each other in the next 6 hours? (CSIR-NET-JUN-2016)

a) 6   b) 7   **c) 11**   d) 12

Total angle in a clock =360^0 , there are 60 minutes , for every minutes the angle will be 360^0/60=6^0

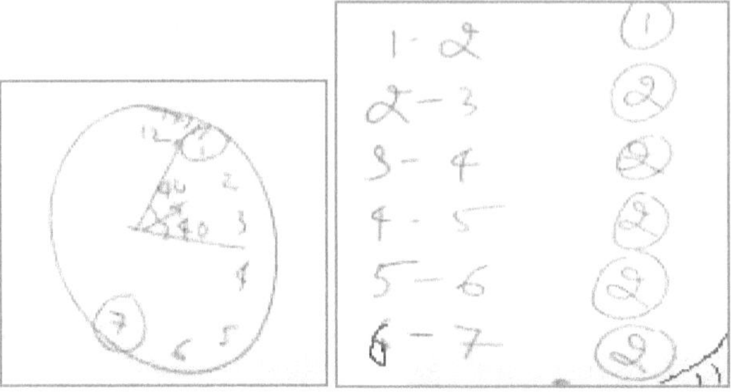

5. At one instant, the hour hand and the minute hand of a clock are one over the other in between the markings for 5 and 6 on the dial. At this instant, the trip of the minute hand.(CSIR-NET-DEC-2015)

a) is closer to the marking for 6
b) is equidistant from the markings for 5 and 6
c) is closer to marking for 5
d) is equidistant from the markings for 11 and 12.
Hint:
We know that angle between hour and minute hand will be 0^0 when they are one over the other i.e. overlap. Angle between hour and minute $(\Theta)=1/2[60H-11M]$, Given H=5, $\Theta= 0^0$
$0=1/2[60x5 – 11M]$ or, M=27(3/11) minutes. Therefore, hour hand and minute hand will be one over another at 5:27:3/11, So, tip of minute hand will be closer to 5.

6. The time gap between the two instants, one before and one after 12: noon, when the angle between the hour hand and the minute hand is 66^0 , is ? (CSIR-NET-JUN-2014)

a) 12 min   b) 16 min   c) 18 min   **d) 24 min**

At 12:00 the value of H=0

7. What is the angle between the minute and hour hand of a clock at 7:35? (CSIR-NET-JUN-2013)

a) 0^0 **b) 17.5^0**   c) 19.5^0 d) 20^0

Hint:

We know that θ = ½| 60H – 11M| =1/2|60*7 – 11*35|=1/2 *35(12 -11) =35/2=17.5

8. At what time after 4 O' clock, the hour and the minute hands will lie opposite in each other? (CSIR-NET-DEC-2012)

a)4-50'-31''   b) 4-52'-51''   c) 4-53'-23''   **d) 4-54'-33''**

Hint:

We know that θ = ½| 60H – 11M|, As **the hour and the minute hands will lie opposite in each, so here** θ = 180

Now θ=1/2|60*4 – 11M|; 180 =1/2|240 – 11M| or, 360=-240 + 11M or, 11M=600 or, M=600/11=54

AVERAGE AND STATISTICS

1. In an exam the average marks for the class was 60, the average of marks of the students who passed was 70 and those failed was 30. What is the percentage of the students of the class who failed?(CSIR-NET-NOV-2020)

a) **25**　　　　b) 40　　　　c) 60　　　　d) 75

Hint:
Suppose, number of students in the class = 100, Average mark of total students = 60, Therefore Total Marks = 60 x 100 = 6000. Let number of passed students = x, so no of failed student =100 –x. As average of passed students=70, therefore, total marks of passed students=70x and total marks of failed students =(100 – x) 30.Now 70x + (100 – x) 30 = 6000 or, 70x +3000-30x=6000 or, 40x = 3000 or x= 75, so no. of failed students =100 –x = 100 – 75 =25.

2. The scores of the six students of Group A in an examination are 38, 45, 42, 58, 62, & 55.In the same examination, the scores of the six students of Group B of size 7 are 38,41,44,46,49 & 52, where one score is missing. If the arithmetic means of the scores of the two groups are same, then what is the missing score? (CSIR-NET-NOV-2020)

a) 80   b) 65   c) 63   d) 62

Hint:

For Group A, Average (A) = (38+45+42+58+62+55) / 6 = 300 / 6 = 50
For Group B, let missing score be x, Average (B) =
(38+41+44+46+49+52+x) / 7 = (270 + x) / 7
As Average two groups are same, therefore (270+x) / 7 = 50 or, 270 + x
=350 or, x = 350 -270 = 80

3. The mean of a set of 10 numbers is M. By combining with it a second set of M numbers, the mean of the combined set becomes 10. What is the sum of the second set of numbers? (CSIR-NET-DEC-2019)

   a) $10M - 1$ b) $10 M + 1$ c) 20   **d) 100**

Hint:
Suppose the 1st set of numbers is x1, x2, x3... x10. Therefore, Mean =
(x1+x2+x3+......+x10) / 10 –M or,
x1+x2+x3+......+x10 = 10M. Suppose the 2nd set of numbers is y1, y2, y3... ym. Now as per question we get,
(x1+x2+x3+...+x10+y1+y2+y3+...+ym)   / (10 + M) = 10 or,
x1+x2+x3+....+x10+y1+y2+y3.....+ym = 10(10 + M).
Or,   x1+x2+x3+....+x10+y1+y2+y3.....+ym   =   100   +10M,   or,
10M+y1+y2+y3+....+ym=100 + 10 M, or,
y1+y2+y3+....+ym = 100+10M-10M = 100.

4. The nine numbers x1, x2, x3..., and x9 are in ascending order. Their average m is strictly greater than all the first eight numbers. Which of the following is true? (CSIR-NET-JUN-2019).

   a)   Average (x1,x2,,...,x9, m) > m and Average (x2,x3,...,x9)> m
   b)   Average (x1,x2,,...,x9, m) < m and Average (x2,x3,...,x9)< m

   c)   **Average (x1,x2,,...,x9, m) = m and Average (x2,x3,...,x9)> m**
   d)   Average (x1,x2,,...,x9, m) <m and Average (x2,x3,...,x9)= m

Hint:

Let x1, x2... x9 are ascending order, therefore Average = (x1+x2+...+x9) / 9 =m, or, x1+x2+...+x9 = 9m

Now Average (x1, x2 ...x9, m) = (x1+x2+...+x9+m) / 10 = (9m + m) /10=10m/10=m,

Again, Average (x2, x3,..., x9) = (x2+x3+...+x9) / 8

As x1<m, x2<m,..., x8<m and Average (x1,...,x9) = m implies that x9>M as Avc(x2,...,x9)≯M

5. Two forest patches have, respectively 100 and 200 teak trees of the same age . In a given season, all trees shed some of their leaves at random. The daily total collections of the leaf litter from the two patches are expected to have: (CSIR-NET-JUN-2019)

   a)   Nearly equal means, standard deviations and coefficients of variation.
   b)   Different means nearly equal standard deviations and coefficients of variations.
   c)   **Different means nearly equal standard deviations and different coefficients of variation.**
   d)   Different means and standard deviations but nearly equal coefficients of variation.

Hint:

Coefficient of variation depends on mean, as it expresses the variation as a percentage of the mean and the mean of average depends on the sample size. So, if the same size is changed here, the means as well as the coefficient of variation is also changed. However, the standard deviation will not vary much; this represents just the dispersion of values about the mean.

6. A student received the following marks in the five of the six courses: 91, 86, 81, 79, and 92. Average of his marks in six subjects is 85. How many marks did he receive in the sixth subject? (CSIR-NET-JUN-2019)

a) 83   b) 85   **c) 81**   d) 88

Hint:

Suppose the student receive marks in the sixth subject=x, Therefore, as per question,

(91+86+81+79+92+x) / 6 =85 or, 91+86+81+79+92+x = 510 or, x= 510-91-86-81-79-92 =510- 429 = 81

7. The average rainfall over a given place during the three-year period of 2003-2005 was 65 cm. During the three-year period 2002-2004 the average rainfall was 63 cm. The actual rainfall during 2005 was 60 cm. What was the rainfall in 2002? (CSIR-NET-DEC-2018)

a)   55cm   b) 60cm   **c) 54cm**   d) 53cm

Hint:

The rainfall in the period 2003-2005 -> 2003+2004+2005=65 x 3 = 195, ------- (i)

Similarly, the rain fall in the period 2002-2004 -> 2002+2003+2004 = 63 x 3 = 189---- (ii)

Now, by doing (i) – (ii) we get, 2005-2002=195-189 = 6 or, 2002 = 6-60 = 54 (Given rainfall in 2002 is 60cm)

8. For the following set of observed values: (60, 65, 65, 70, 70, 70, 70, 82, 85, 90, 95, 100, 160,160), Which of the statements is true? (CSIR-NET-DEC-2018)

a)   **Mode<median<mean**   b) mode < mean < median   c) mean<median<mode   d) median<mode<mean

Hint:

Sorted data set in descending order: 160, 160, 100, 95, 95, 90, 85, 82, 70, 70, 70, 70, 65, 65, 60

Mean=The total sum of numbers divided by total frequencies of these numbers. Therefore,

Mean=

{(1x60)+(2x65)+(4x70)+(1x82)+(1x85)+(1x90)+(2x95)+(1x100)+(2x160)} / (1+2+4+1+1+1+2+1+2)

= (60+130+280+82+85+90+190+100+320) / 15 = 1337/15 = **89.13**

(The number of times a value occurs in a set of values is it's frequency which is 15 here)

Mode: The mode is the number with the highest frequency (when the frequency is at-least 2 or more).
Mode= **70** (as it has 4 frequency which is also highest)
Median: The median of a set of numbers is the one lying in the exact middle of the sequence.(For odd number of numbers , the middle position refers to the (number of numbers – 1) / 2. So, in this case (15 - 1) / 2 =7. So here we need to find the number at the 7th position and which 82 are.

9. The distance between X and Y is 1000km. A person flies from X at 8 AM local time and reaches Y at 10 AM local time. He flies back after a halt of 4 hours at Y and reaches X at 4 PM local time on the same day. What is his average speed for the duration he is in the air? (CSIR-NET-DEC-2016)

a) 500 km/hour   b) 250 km/hour   c) 750 km/hour   d) cannot be calculated with the given information.

Hint: Distance between X and Y =1000 km and also distance from Y to X =1000km .The total distance travel =1000 + 1000=2000km. The time taken from 8 am to 10 am =2 hour and also the time taken from 2 pm to 4pm=2 hour(after halting 4 hrs , he started from Y at 2 pm and reaches X at 4 pm). The total time taken for up and down =2 hour + 2 hour = 4 hour. Average Speed = Total distance / Total time = 2000 / 4 =500 km/hour

10. The set of numbers (5, 6, 7, m, 6, 7, 8, n) has an arithmetic mean of 6 and mode (most frequently occurring number) of 7. The m x n =? (CSIR-NET-JUN-2016)

   a)   18   b) 35   c) 28   **d) 14**

Hint:
Average of Mean or Arithmetic Mean (M) = sum of elements / total number of elements
M = (5+6+7+m+6+7+n) / 8 =6 or, 5+6+7+m+6+7+8+n =48 or, m+n = 48-39 = 9
Given that mode= 7, so, at least either m or n must be 7. Suppose m =7 and, so n will be 9-7=2 and as a result mxn =7 x 2 =14.

11. A student appearing for an exam is declared to have failed the exam if his / her score is less than half the median score. This implies? (CSIR-NET-JUN-2016)

   a) ¼ of the students appearing for the exam always fail.
   b) If a student scores less than ¼ of the maximum score, he/she always fails.
   c) If a student scores more than ½ of the maximum score, he/she always passes.
   d) It is possible that no one fails.

   Hint:
   By definition of median, it is a number which divides the given group in two equal parts. So, option a), b) and c) cannot satisfy in each case , while option d) can be possible.

12. If you change only one observation from a set of 10 observations, which of the following will definitely changes? (CSIR-NET-JUN-2015)

   a) Mean   b) Median   c) Mode   d) Standard Deviation
Hint:

Mean (M) = (sum of observations) / (Total number of observations)
If we change only 1 observation, the sum of observations will also change definitely. Thus, Mean will definitely change if there is change in only o observation.

13. Weights (in kg) of 13 persons are: 70, 72, 74, 76, 78, 80, 82, 84, 86, 88, 90, 92, and 94. Two new persons having weights 100 kg and 79 kg join the group. The average weight of the group increases by ?(CSIR-NET-DEC-2014)

   a) 0 kg   **b) 1 kg**   c) 1.6 kg   d) 1.8 kg

Hint:
 Average   weights   of   13   persons   =
(70+72+74+76+78+80+82+84+86+88+90+92+94) / 13 = 1066 / 13 = 82

Average   weights   of   15   persons   =
(70+72+74+76+78+80+82+84+86+88+90+92+94+100+79)   /   15   =
1245/15=83.

So, the average weight of the group increases by 1 kg(83kg-82kg=1kg).

14. Students in a group a obtained the following marks: 40, 80, 70, 50, 60, 90, 30. Students in group B obtained: 40, 80, 35, 70, 85, 45, 50, 75, 60 marks. Define Dispersion (D)= (maximum marks – minimum marks), and Relative Dispersion (RD) = Dispersion / Mean, Then ? (CSIR-NET-JUN-2014)

a) RD of group A = Rd of group B   **b) RD of group A > RD of group B**

c) RD of group A < RD of group B   d) D of group A< D of group B

Hint:

For group A, Dispersion = Maximum Marks – Minimum Marks = 90 – 30 = 60 and Mean= (40+80+70+50+60+90+30) / 7 = 420/7= 60, Now, Relative Dispersion = Dispersion / Mean = 60/60=1

For group B, Dispersion = Maximum Marks – Minimum Marks = 85 – 35 = 50 and Mean=(40+80++35+70+85++45+50+75+60) / 9 = 540/9= 60 , Now , Relative Dispersion = Dispersion / Mean = 50/60=5/6=.83

15. What is the arithmetic mean of 1/ (1x2) , 1/(2x3), 1/(3x4),1/(4x5),..., 1/(100x101) ?(CSIR-NET-DEC-2013)

a) 0.01   **b) 1/101**   c) 0.00111....   d) 1/(49x50) + 1/(50x51)

Hint:

1/ (1x2)= 1/1 – ½   , 1/(2x3) =1/2 – 1/3 , 1/(3x4)= 1/3 – ¼ , 1/(4x5)= ¼ - 1/5 , ..., 1/(100x101=1/100 – 1/101, So we get 100 terms in the sequence.

Therefore, Arithmetic Mean ={ 1/ (1x2)+1/(2x3)+1/(3x4)+1/(4x5)+...+1/(100x101)}/100
=(1/1-1/2+1/2-1/3-1/3-1/4+1/4-1/5+.....+1/100-1/101)/100 =(1/1-1/101)/100 =(101-1/101)100=(100/101)/100
=(100/101)x(1/100)=1/101

16. Suppose the sum of the seven positive numbers is 21. What is the minimum possible value of the average of the squares of these numbers? (CSIR-NET-DEC-2012)

a) 63   b) 21   **c) 9**   d) 7

Hint: As the sum of the seven positive numbers is 21 , so the average of the number=21/7=3 , so the numbers are 3,3,3,3,3,3,3. Thus the minimum possible value of the average of squares of these numbers =(9+9+9+9+9+9+9)/ 7 = 63/7=9

(We know that Arithmetic Progression >= Geometrical Progression. When all numbers are equal then AP=GP.
If two or more positive numbers whose sum is constant, then the square of numbers will be minimum when the numbers are equal.)

17. Let A=$(1^{13} + 2^{13}+3^{13}+...+100^{13})$/100 , B=$(1^{13}+3^{13}+5^{13}+...+99^{13})$/50 and C =$(2^{13}+4^{13}+6^{13}+...+100^{13})$/50
Which of the following is true?(CSIR-NET-DEC-2012)

a) B<C<A   b) A<B<C   **c) B<A<C**   d) C<A<B

Hint:
Both B and C have the same denominator and in numerator of B, each of the terms is less than the corresponding term in the numerator of C. $1^{13}<2^{13}$, $3^{13}<4^{13}$...$99^{13}<100^{13}$, therefore, we can say B<C.
Now B+C=$(1^{13}+3^{13}+5^{13}+...+99^{13})$/50 + $(2^{13}+4^{13}+6^{13}+...+100^{13})$/50 = $(1^{13} + 2^{13}+3^{13}+...+100^{13})$/50, So we can say that B + C = 2A (As A=$(1^{13} + 2^{13}+3^{13}+...+100^{13})$/100, So, 2A = 2 x $(1^{13} + 2^{13}+3^{13}+...+100^{13})$/100 =$(1^{13} + 2^{13}+3^{13}+...+100^{13})$/50)

As, A=(B+C)/2 , that is A is the Arithmetic Mean of B and C.(The value of Arithmetic Mean is always in between the numbers). Hence , B<A<C.

<u>YEAR, WEEK, DAY</u>

1.Which of the following months in 2021 will have the same calendar (the same days and dates) as that in Sept 2020?(CSIR-NET-NOV-2020)

    a) March   b) April   c) November   **d) June**

Hint:
Two months will have same calendar (the same days and dates), if number of odd days between them are 0 (i.e. multiple of 7).
In September 2020 - 2 odd days
October 2020 – 3 odd days
November 2020 – 2 odd days

December 2020 – 3 odd days
January 2021 – 3 odd days
February 2021 – 0 odd days
March 2021 – 3 odd days
April 2021 – 2 odd days
May 2021 – 3 odd days
Hence between September 2020 and December 2020 number of odd days are 0, but they have asked a month in year 2021. Number of odd days between September 2020 and June 2021 are 0(21=multiple of 7).

2. If the day after tomorrow is NOT Friday then which of the following day CANNOT be the day before the day before yesterday? (CSIR-NET-NOV-2020).

    a) **Sunday**   b) Monday   c) Tuesday   d) Wednesday

Hint:
The day after tomorrow is Friday. Then today is Wednesday. Yesterday was Tuesday. Day before yesterday was Monday. Day before the day before yesterday was Sunday. Therefore, if tomorrow is NOT Friday, then day before the day before yesterday CANNOT be Sunday.

3. What day of the week will it be 61 days from a Friday? (CSIR-NET-NOV-2020)

    a) Saturday   b) Sunday   c) Friday   **d) Wednesday**

Hint:
Each day of the week is repeated after 7 days. So, after 61 days, 5 odd days will be there. If today is Friday, after 5 day it will be Wednesday.

4. A Certain Day which is X Days before 17th August, is such that 50 days prior to that day, it was 4x Days since March 30th of the same Year. What is X? (CSIR-NET-DEC-2014)

a) **18**   b) 30   c) 22   d) 16

Hint:

Given two dates, 30th March and 17th August are given and some dates in between these two dates are given in terms of an unknown variable x. We need to find the value of x.

The number of days from 30th March to 17th August as below:

31st March = 1 day, April =30 days, May=31 days, June=30 days, July=31 days, August=17 days

I.e. 1+30+31+30+31+17=140 days

Thus 30th March as the 0th day and 17th August as the 140th day .,

Therefore 4x + 50 + x=140 , or, 5x=90or,x=18

5. If a 4-digit year (e.g.1927) is chosen randomly, what is the probability that it is NOT a leap year?(CSIR-NET-JUN-2014)

a) ¾   b) ¼   c) <1/4   **d) >3/4**

Hint:

We know that for a year to be leap year, there are two conditions: i) it should be divisible by 4 ii) If it is divisible by 100, it should also be divisible by 400.

In every 4 consecutive no's, there will be three numbers that are not divisible by 4.So, as per condition i) ,Chances for a randomly chosen year to be non-leap year is ¾. And as per condition ii), more years become non-leap years. So our answer is >3/4.

For better understanding, we may take example of four consecutive years 1899,1900,1901,1902 in which no leap year occurs. By condition i), 1899, 1901, 1902 are non-leap years. Again by the condition ii) , 1900 is also a non-leap year. So, in the above 4 years, the probability of non-leap years is 1; which is greater than ¾.

6. November 9, 1994 was a Wednesday. Then which of the following is true? (CSIR-NET-JUN-2014)

    i)   November 9, 1965 is a Wednesday and November 9, 1970 is a Wednesday.

    ii)   November 9, 1965 is not a Wednesday and November 9, 1970 is a Wednesday.

    iii)   November 9, 1965 is a Wednesday and November 9, 1970 is not a Wednesday.

iv)   November 9, 1965 is not a Wednesday and November 9, 1970 is not a Wednesday.

Hint:

We have to determine (1) the number of odd days in between November 9, 1970 and November 9, 1994

And also (2) in between November 9, 1965 and November 9, 1994.

For case (1), there are 24 complete years between these two dates. So there are total 6 leap years and 24-6=18 non-leap years. We know that every leap-year has 2 odd days and every non-leap year have 1 odd day i.e. (6 x 2) + (18 x 1) = 30(mod7)=2 odd days. Reference day is Wednesday, so November 9, 1970 will be Monday (subtract 2 days from Reference day).

 For case (2) ,there are 29 complete years between these two dates. So, there are total 7 leap year and 29-7=22 non-leap years i.e. (7 x 2) + (22 x 1)= 36 (mod7) =1 odd day. As the reference day is Wednesday, so November 9, 1965 is Tuesday. So, option iv) is correct.

7. What is the maximum sum of the number of Saturday and Sunday in a leap year? (CSIR-NET-DEC-2013)

a) 104   b) 105   **c) 106**   d) 107

Hint:

In a leap year, there are total 366 days, i.e. 52 complete weeks and 2 odd days, so, there are 52 Saturdays and 52 Sundays which sums to 104 days. To maximize the sum of the number of Saturdays and Sundays, we can consider that the two odd days be Saturday and Sunday respectively. So maximum sum of the number of Saturdays and Sundays = 104 + 2 = 106.

8. What is the minimum number of days between one Friday the 13th and the next Friday the 13th? (CSIR-NET-DEC-2012)

a) 28   b) 56   **c) 91**   d) 84

Hint:

In a leap year, February has 29 days. Assume that 13th of the given year falls on a Friday.AS a day gets repeated after every 7 days, the next

Friday of another month if the number of days counted from January 13th till the 13th of that month is a multiple of 7.

Jan 13th to Feb 13th =31, which is not a multiple of 7.

Jan 13th to Mar 13th = 31 + 29 =60, which is not a multiple of 7.

Jan 13th to Apr 13th = 31 + 29 + 31 = 91, , which is multiple of 7. So, option c) is correct.

PROFIT, LOSS, DISCOUNT

1. A bank pays interest to its depositors compounded yearly. If a deposit becomes Rs.54000/- at the end of 3rd year and Rs.64800/- at the end of 6th year, what is the principal invested in the deposit? (CSIR-NET-NOV-2020)

a) 40000   b) 42500   **c) 45000**   d) 48000

Hint:

Let P be the principal amount and R be the rate of interest, then after 3 years, n=3, we have

$54000 = P (1+R/100)^3$ or, $(54000)^2 = P^2(1+R/100)^6$------- (i)

After 6 years, n= 6, we have $64800= P (1+R/100)^6$ ...... (ii)
Now, (i) / (ii), $(54000)^2 / 64800 = \{ P^2(1+R/100)^6 / P(1+R/100)^6 \}$ or, P = $(54000)^2 / 64800 = (54000 \times 54000) / 64800$
Or, P = 45000

2. A precious stone breaks into four pieces having weights in the proportion 1:2:3:4. The value of such a stone is proportional to the square of its weight. What is the percent loss in the value incurred due to breaking?(CSIR-NET-JUN-2019)

    a) 0   b) 30   **c) 70**   d) 90

Hint:

Suppose the common factor of the proportion is x. Therefore, the weights of the stone will be 1x + 2x + 3x + 4x =10x. The Value of stone is proportional to the square of the weight which are $1x^2, 4 x^2, 9 x^2, 16 x^2$. The total value of broken stone = $1x^2+4 x^2+9 x^2+16 x^2=30x^2$. Value of unbroken stone ∞ (weight of stone)^2 = $(10x)^2$ = $100x^2$. The % loss of Value of stone = $\{(CP-SP) / CP\}$ 100= $\{ (100x^2 - 30x^2)/ 100x^2 \}$ 100= 70%

3. Salesperson 'A' sells an object at a price Rs.5 less than the marked price, receiving a commission of 5% on the selling price. The same object is sold by person 'B' at a price Rs. 15 less than the marked price, receiving a commission of 15% on the selling price. If both A and B receive the same amount in commission, then what is the marked price of the object? (CSIR-NET-JUN-2019)

    a) 10   **b) 20**   c) 22.5   d) 30

Hint:

Let the marked price = x. Now A sell the object at price Rs.(x-5) and receives commission Rs.5(x-5)/100.
Similarly, B sell the object at a price Rs(x-15) and receives commission Rs.15(x-15)/100. As per question, 15(x-15)/100 = 5(x-5)/100 or, 15(x-15) =5(x-5) or, 15x -225 = 5x -25 or, 15x − 5x =225-25=200 or, 10x=200 or. x= 20

4. A man buys alcohol at Rs.75/cl, adds water, and sells it at Rs. 75/cl making a profit of 50%. What is the ratio of alcohol to water? (CSIR-NET-DEC-2016)

    a)   2:1   b) 1:2   c) 3:2   d) 2:3

Hint:

Here CP=Rs.75/cl , Profit=50% , So, SP = (CP + 50% of Cp)=75+37.5=112.5 , Therefore quantity sold = 112.5/75=1.5 i.e. 1 lit alcohol with .5 lit water , Therefore the ratio of alcohol :water=1:0.5 = 2:1

5. A vendor sells articles having a cost price of Rs.100 each. He sells these articles at a premium price during the first eight months, and at a sale price, which is half of the premium price, during the next four months. He makes a net profit of 20% at the end of the year. Assuming that equal numbers of articles are sold each month, what is the premium price of the article? (CSIR-NET-DEC-2016)

    a)   122   **b) 144**   c) 150   d) 160

Hint:

Suppose the premium price of sell =Rs. x and so, sell price =Rs. x/2. Let us assume that each month, the vendor sold 1 article then he sold 8 + 4 = 12 article in 12 month. Therefore, the total Selling Price (S.P) for the first 8 months = no. of articles sold x price of each article = 8x. Similarly Total selling price of last four month = 4x/2=2x. So, the total S.P for 12 month = 8x + 2x =10x. Now the Cost Price = 100 x 12 = 1200. Therefore Profit will be = (20/100)1200 = 240. As profit =S.P – C.P, So, 10x -1200 =240 , or 10x = 240+1200=1440 or, x=1440/10=144.

6. A shopkeeper purchases a product for Rs.100 and sells it making a profit of 10%. The customer results it to the same shopkeeper incurring a loss of 10%. In these dealings the shopkeeper makes? (CSIR-NET-DEC-2015)

a) No profit no loss   **b) Rs.11**   c) Rs.1   d) Rs.20

Hint:

In first case, Shopkeeper's profit =10% of 100 =10, so sell price will be 110. In second case customer's cost price =110 and loss of customer =10% of 110 = (10/100)110= 11, so the sale price =110-11=99, here shopkeeper's profit=1 . So the total profit of shopkeeper = 10+1=11

7. A student buys a book from an online shop at 20% discount. His friend buys another copy of the same book in a book fair for Rs.192 paying 20% less than his friend. What is the full price of the books?(CSIR-NET-Jun-2015)

a) Rs.275   **b) Rs.300**   c) Rs.320   d) Rs.392

Hint:

Let the full price of the book is Rs.x. Now the student buys the book at 20% discount i.e. he buys the book at price of Rs.{x-(20/100)x}=x – x/5 = 4x/5. His friend buys the same book at Rs.192 which is 20% less than the student i.e. he purchases the book at price of Rs.{4x/5 – (4x/5)(20/100)} = 4x/5 – 4x/25 =(20x – 4x)/25 = 16x/25. So, as per question 16x/25= 192 or 16x= 192 * 25 or, x= 192*25/16 =12*25=300. Hence the full price of the book is Rs. 300.

8. A person sells two objects at Rs.1035/- each. On the first object, he suffers a loss of 10% while on the second he gains 15%. What is his net loss / gain percentage? (CSIR-NET-DEC-2014)

a) 5% gain   **b) <1% gain**   c) < 1% less   d) no loss, no gain

Hint:

Let the Cost price of the 1st object=x , and 2nd object=y. In 1st object Loss% = {(C.P – S.P) / C.P}*100 ={(x-1035) / x}*100 which is 10% i.e. 10

=$\{(\ x-1035\ )\ /\ x\}*100$ Or, $10x=100x - 103500$ or, $90x =103500$ or, $x=1150$. In case of 2nd object Gain% = $\{(S.P - C.P)/C.P\}*100$ Or, $15 = \{(1035 - y)/y\}*100$ or, $15y = 103500-100y$ or, $115y=103500$ or, $y= 900$. The total sale price = $1035+1035 = 2070$ and total Cost price = $1150+900=2050$ and the profit = $2070-2050=20$. Net Gain %=$\{(S.P - C.P)/C.P\}*100$ = $\{(2070-2050)/2050\}*100$ = $20*100/2050=2000/2005=0.98<1$.

9. A merchant buys equal numbers of shirts and trousers and pays Rs.38000. If the cost of 3 shirts is Rs.800 and that of a trouser is Rs. 1000, then how many shirts were bought? (CSIR-NET-JUN-2014)

a) 60   **b) 30**   c) 15   d) 10

Hint:

Let the merchant buys x number of shirts and trousers each. Then as per question,
$X*800/3 + x* 1000 =38000$ or, $(800x+3000x) / 3 =38000$ or, $3800x = 38000*3$ or $x= (38000*3) / 3800=30$

10. After giving a 20% discount on the marked price to a customer, the seller's profit was 20%. Which of the following is true? (CSIR-NET-JUN-2014)

a)   Sale price = (Marked price + Cost price)/ 2
b)   **Sale price < (Marked price + Cost price)/ 2**
c) 2(Marked price + Cost price)/ 3 > Sale price > (Marked price + Cost price)/ 2
d) Sale price >2 (Marked price + Cost price)/ 3

Hint:
Let the marked price =100, so the sale price will be 100-20=80, Now the Profit % =(sale Price −cost price)*100/cost price or, 20 =(80 − cost price)*100/cost price or, 20*cost price =8000-100*cost price,
Or,120*cost price=8000 or, cost price =8000/120 =66.66, Now , (Marked Price + Cost Price)/2 =166.66/2=83.33 which is > sale price i.e. Sale Price < (Marked Price + Cost Price)/2.

11. You get 20% returns on your investment annually, but also pay a 20% tax on the gain. At the end of 5 years, the net gain made by you (as percentage of the capital) is approximately.(CSIR-NET-JUN-2014)

a) 0   b) 16   **c) 80**   d) 100

Hint:

 Pay tax 20% on return of 20% annually= 20*20/100=4% i.e. net return =20% - 4% =16 % annually. So in the end of 5 years, the net gain will be 5*16%=80%

12. A fruit vendor buys 120 Shimla apples at 4 for Rs.100 and 120 Golden apples at 6 for Rs.100. She decides to mix them and sell at 10 for rs.200. She will make? (CSIR-NET-DEC-2012)

a) No profit no loss   **b) a loss of 4%**   c) a gain of 4%   d) a loss of 10%

Hint:

The cost price of Shimla apples = (100/4) =25 per apple or the total cost of 120 shimla apples =120*25=3000 and also the cost price of Golden apples =100/6 or the total cost price =(100/6)*120=2000. Now the total cost of 120Shimla apples and 120Golden apples = 3000 + 2000=5000, so the cost price of (120+120=240) mixed apple =5000. Now the sell price for 10 apples=200 , so the sale price for 240 apples = 200*240/10=4800. Now the Loss%= (C.P –S.P)*100/C.P= (5000 – 4800)*100/5000 =200*100/5000=4%

PROBABILITY

1. Four babies born in the month of April 2019 are randomly selected. The probability that at least two of them will have the same date of birth is? (CSIR-NET-NOV-2020)

a)81.2%   **b)18.8%**   c)13.7%
d)86.3%

Hint:

Total outcomes to be born of four babies in the month of April 2019 i.e. 30days =n(s) = $^{30}C_1$ x $^{30}C_1$ x $^{30}C_1$ x $^{30}C_1$

Number of outcomes to be born of all four babies on different dates=n(a)= $^{30}C_1$ x $^{29}C_1$ x $^{28}C_1$ x $^{27}C_1$

Now, all babies born on different dates (P)= n(a)/n(s) = 30x29x28x27 / 30x30x30x30 = 21924/27000

Now, at least two of them will have same date of birth= 1 −P=1 − 21924/27000=5076/27000 =188/1000=0.188

Therefore % required is =18.8%

2. The probability distribution of weights of a certain population is normal as shown in the figure. What is the probability that the weight of a person picked at random is more than 60 kg? (CSIR-NET-NOV-2020)

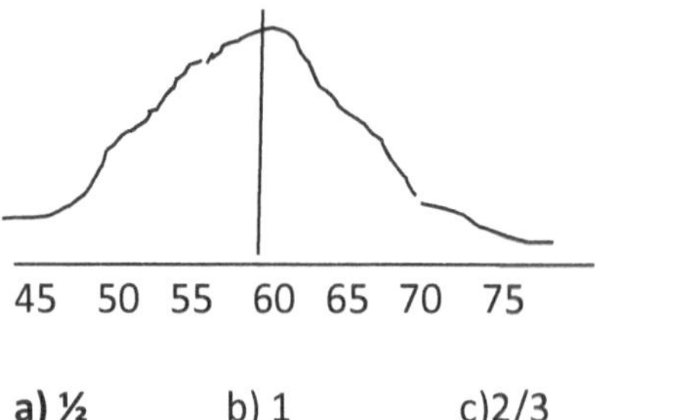

a) ½   b) 1   c)2/3   d) 1/3

Hint:
From the graph it is clear that there are 50% people having weights less than 60 kg and 50% people having more than 60 kg weights.Therefore, P (weight of a person randomly picked is more than 60 kg =1/2

3. The probability that team A wins a match against team B is 2/3. If teams A and B play 4 matches against each other, what is the probability that team A will win at least one match? (Assume that result od one match does not influence the rest.)(CSIR-NET-NOV-2020).

a) 2/3   b) 4/9   c) 1   **d) 80/81**

Hint:
Probability of wining of a match by team A = 2/3 , Probability of losing a match by team A =1 − 2/3 =1/3

Total 4 matches are played . Probability (of wining at least one match by team A)= 1 –P(winning no match by team A)=1- (1/3 x 1/3 x 1/3 x 1/3) =1- 1/81 = 80/81.

4. A marksman had four successes in six attempts. What is the probability that he had three consecutive successes? (CSIR-NET-NOV-2020)

a) 9/15   b) 12/15   c) 13/15   d) 6/15

Hint:
Here sample space is
S=(FFSSSS,SFFSSS,SSFFSS,SSSFFS,SSSSSFF,FSSSSF,FSFSSS,FSSFSS,FSSSFS,SFSFSS,SFSSFS,SFSSSF,SSFSFS,SSSFSF,SSFSSF)
Event = (FFSSSS, SFFSSS, SSSFFS, SSSSFF, FSSSSSF, SFSSSF, FSFSSS, FSSSFS, SSSFSF)
Therefore, probability (of three consecutive success) =9/15

5. A multiple choice has 4 questions each with 4 answers choices. Every question has only one correct answer. The probability of getting all answer correct by independent random Guesses for each one is ? (CSIR-NET-DEC-2019)

a) ¼   **b) $(¼)^4$**   c) ¾   d) $(3/4)^4$

The probability of correct answer of question no. 1 is ¼
The probability of correct answer of question no. 2 is ¼ and so on.
Therefore probability of random guesses is ¼ x ¼ x ¼ x ¼ =$(1/4)^4$
If wrong answer then the probability will be (3/4). If three are 3 correct and one is wrong then the answer will be ¼ x1/4 x ¼ x3/4

6. 12 balls, 3 each of the colour red, green; blue and yellow are put in a box and mixed. If 3 balls are picked at random, without replacement, the probability that all 3 balls are of the same colour is? (CSIR-NET-DEC-2019)

a) ¼   b) 1/12   c) 1/36   **d) 1/55**

RRR   GGG   BBB   YYY

Here THE PROBABILITY OF RRR = $^{3}C_{3}$ GGG= $^{3}C_{3}$ and so on……
RRR + GGG + BBB + YYY = $^{3}C_{3}/^{12}C_{3}$ + $^{3}C_{3}/^{12}C_{3}$ + $^{3}C_{3}/^{12}C_{3}$ + $^{3}C_{3}/^{12}C_{3}$
=1/220 +1/220 +1/220+1/220
=4/220 =55.
Alternate:
Red : Probability of getting first ball as red =3/12 [P(Event)=Number of successful outcome/ Total number of possible outcomes]
: Probability of getting second ball as red =2/11(here successful outcomes now is 2 because 1 red ball is already taken and remaining total balls in box is 11)
: Probability of getting third ball as red =1/10
So, the probability of getting all 3 balls as red =3/12 x 2/11 x 1/11=1/220

So, probability of getting all 3 balls as blue=1/220, probability of getting all 3 balls as green=1/220 and probability of getting all 3 balls as yellow =1/220
 So, probability of getting either of all 3as red, green, blue or yellow= 1/220 x 1/220 x 1/220 x 1/220 = 1/55

7. Out of 6 unbiased coins, 5 are tossed independently and they all results in heads. If the 6th is now independently tossed, the probability of getting heads is? (CSIR-NET-DEC-2018)

a) 1   b) 0   **c) ½**   d) 1/6

Hint:

Total number of outcomes when 6th coin is tossed =2 (either Head or Tail)
Number of outcome in which head comes= 1 (because other outcome is Tall)
Probability of getting Head = Number of outcomes (in which Head Comes/ Total number of outcomes= 1/2

8. Two students are solving the same problem independently. If the probability that the first one solves the problem is 3/5 and the probability that the second solves the problem is 4/5. What is the probability that at least one of them solves the problem? (CSIR-NET-JUN-2018)

   a)   17/25   b) 19/25   c)21/25   **d) 23/25**
Hint:

Probability of First one to solve problem = 3/5 , So, Probability of First one not to solve problem = 1-3/5=2/5
Probability of second one to solve problem = 4/5 , Probability of Second one not to solve problem = 1-4/5=1/5
 Probability of at least one to solve the problem = 1- probability of none to solve = 1- (2/5 * 1/5)= 1-2/25=23/25

9. A fair die was thrown three times and the outcome was repeatedly six. If the die is thrown again, what is the probability of getting six? (CSIR-NET-JUN-2017)

a) 1/6   b) 1/213   c) 1/1296   d) 1

In a die, there are 1, 2, 3, 4, 5, 6. So the probability of getting six is always 1/6.
Since throwing a die is a random, any number of die thrown won't change the probability of a particular event. So, we just need to find out the probability of 6 in a die and that is 1/6.

10. Three boxes are coloured red, blue and green and so is three balls. In how many ways can one put the balls one in each box such that no ball goes into the box of its own colour? (CSIR-NET-DEC-2015)

a) 1   **b) 2**   c) 3   d) 4

R	B	G
B	G	R

R	B	G
G	R	B

11. The probability that a ticketless traveller is caught during a trip is 0.1. If the traveller makes 4 trips, the probability that he/she will be caught during at least one of the trip is? (CSIR-NET-DEC-2015)

a) 1-(0.9)^4   b) (1-0.9)^4 c) 1-(1-0.9)^4 d) (0.9)^4

The probability of not caught =1 – 0.1 =0.9   therefore for 4 times not caught =1-(0.9)^4
If it is said at least then it will be 1- not caught 4 times
[The probability of caught=0.1 , The total probability is always 1.
So, the probability of not caught in 1st trip = 1 -0.1=0.9
So, the probability of not caught in 2nd trip = 1 -0.1=0.9
So, the probability of not caught in 3rd trip = 1 -0.1=0.9
So, the probability of not caught in 4th trip = 1 -0.1=0.9
Therefore, the probability of getting caught in none of the 4 trips= 0.9 x .09 x 0.9 x 0.9 =(0.9)^4
So, the probability of getting caught in at least one of the trip = 1 -(0.9)^4

12. Students of a school are divided into 4 groups. What is the probability that friends get into the same group? (CSIR-NET-DEC-2013)

a) ¾   b) 1/64   **c) 1/16**   d) 1/3

The probability to be in one group out of four group is ¼, as 3 students will be in same group then the probability will be
A   B   C   D →   ¼ ¼ ¼ + ¼ ¼ ¼ + ¼ ¼ ¼ + ¼ ¼ ¼ =4 x ¼ ¼ ¼ = 1/16

[Let B1, B2, B3 are three friends and P, Q, R, S are four groups.
The probability of B1 getting into group P = ¼; Similarly, The probability of B2 getting into group P = ¼
And the probability of B3 getting into group P = ¼; Then, probability that the three friends get into group
P = ¼ x ¼ x ¼. As there are four groups, probability that the three friends get into any one of these groups = 4 x (¼ x ¼ x ¼) = 1/16]

13. _Two integers are picked at random from the first 15 positive integers without replacement. What is the probability that the sum of the two numbers is 20? (CSIR-NET-JUN-2013)

a) ¾   **b) 1/21**   c) 1/105   d) 1/20

Hint: (5,15) ;(6,14); (7,13);(8,12) ;(9,11)   = 5 / $^{15}C_2$ = 1/21

[Probability = Number of successful outcomes / Total number of possible outcomes. Now, total number of possible outcomes, that means, number of ways in which two positive integers can be selected from 15positive integers = $^{15}C_2$= (15 x 14) / 2 =105.

Now , the possible pairs for which the sum is 20 is (5,15),(6,14),(7,13),(8,12),(9,11) , that means , there are 5 such pairs. So, the number of successful outcomes =5, Thus the Probability=5/105 = 1/21]

14. A point is chosen at random from a circular disc shown in the figure. What is the probability that the point lies in the sector OAB?

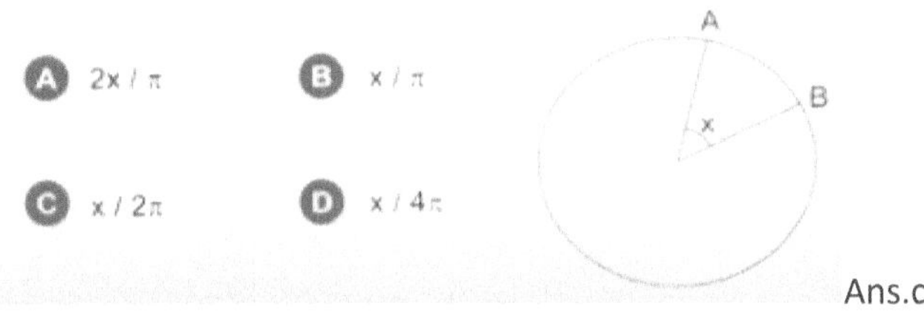

A 2x / π   **B** x / π

C x / 2π   **D** x / 4π

Ans.c

Hint: The formula of area of sector in a circle = x/360 πr^2 and the area of a circle is $\pi r^{2,}$ Therefore,x/360 πr^2/ πr^2 = x/360 = x/ 2π

[Area of a sector=(n/360)πr^2 ,where n= Degree of the central angle of the sector. Here n=x

In order to find out the probability, we just need to find the shares of the sector OAB = Area of sector OAB / Area of Circle

= (πr^2x/360)/ πr^2 = x/360= x/2 π]

PERMUTATION AND COMBINATION

1.In a legislative assembly of 250 members, political parties A, B, C, D and E got 100,70,48,15,7 seats, respectively, while 10 seats were won by the independents. If parties A, B and C decide not to support each other, what is the minimum number of political parties required to join hands to form a majority government?

a) One   b) Two   **c) Three**   d) Four

Hint:

For majority Government, total numbers of seats required 50% of total seat + 1 = (250/2) + 1 =126 seats.
The only possible political parties required joining hands & making 126 + seats are A, D, E & Independent seats. But Independent seats are not political party. Therefore minimum numbers of political parties are 3.

2. At a book-signing session, there are 5 authors who write only single – author books and another 5 who write only in pairs. Every author signs books that are authored or co-authored by him/her. In order to collect signatures of all 10 authors, in the best possible scenario, the minimum number of books that need to be purchased is ? (CSIR-NET-NOV-2020)

a)   5   b) 6   **c) 8**   d) 10

Hint:
Choose those 5 books which are single author books written by 5 different authors and choose 3 books which are written in pair and by different 5 authors. Therefore minimum number of books is 8.

3. Which of the following words can be formed using only the letters of the word "FLOCCINAUCINIHILIPILIFICATION"? When forming a word you can use a letter at most as many times as it appears in the above word? (CSIR-NET-NOV-2020)

a)PHILOPPINES   b) CHINCHILLA   **c) CINCINNATI** d) NATIONALITY

Hint:
The given word contains letters F- 2 times , L-3 times, O – 2 times , C- 4 times, I – 9 times ,N-3 times, A – 2 times , U – 1 time, H- 1 time , P-1 time , T – 1 time.
 Now option a) contains P – 3 times (Incorrect as in original word there is P-1 time)
Option b) contains H- 2 times (Incorrect as in original word there is H-1 time)
Option c) contains C-2 times, I- 3 times, N-3 times, A-1time, T-1time (Correct as in original word there is C-3 time,I-9 times,N-3 times, A- 2 times,T-1 time)
Option d) contains T- 2 times (Incorrect as in original word there is T-1 time)

4. Suppose there are 6 non-stop flights from Chennai to Mumbai in the morning and 4 non-stop flights from Mumbai to Goa in the evening. In how many ways can one fly from Chennai to Goa via Mumbai using these flights in days? (CSIR-NET-NOV-2020)

a) 10   **b) 24**   c) 4^6 d) 6^4

Hint:

Chennai to Mumbai: $^6C_1$ and Mumbai to Goa $^4C_1$. There for total ways $=^6C_1 * {}^4C_1 = 6 \times 4 = 24$

5. A bag contains 8 red balls, 10 blue balls, 17 green balls. What is the minimum number of balls that needs to be taken out from the bag to ensure getting at least one ball of each other? (CSIR-NET-DEC-2019)

    a)   19   b) 18   c) 28   d) 27

Hint:

Firstly, we take 8 red balls after that 10 blue balls, then the only possible ball that we have to take is Green. Therefore, minimum numbers of balls are 8+10+1 = 19 .

6. How many different salads can be made from cauliflower, tomatoes, onions, potatoes and carrots? ?(CSIR-NET-DEC-2018)

a) 16   b) 28   **c) 31**   d) 32

Hint:

$^nC_r = n! / r!(n-r)!$ Here , $^5C_1 + {}^5C_2 + {}^5C_3 + {}^5C_4 + {}^5C_5 = 5/1 + (5 \times 4) / (2 \times 1) + (5 \times 4 \times 3) / (3 \times 2 \times 1) + (5 \times 4 \times 3 \times 2) / (4 \times 3 \times 2 \times 1) + (5 \times 4 \times 3 \times 2 \times 1) / (5 \times 4 \times 3 \times 2 \times 1) = 5 + 10 + 10 + 5 + 1 = 31$

7. In a group of 11 persons, each shakes hands with every other once and only once. What is the total number of such handshakes? (CSIR-NET-JUN-2018)

a)110   b) 121   **c) 55**   d)66

Hint:

$^{n}C_2 = {}^{11}C_2 = 11 \times 10/1 \times 2 = 55$ ($^{n}C_r = n!/r!(n-r)!$ (Alternatively , Total hand shake $= 10+9+8+7+6+5+4+3+2+1 = 55$)

8. In how many ways can you place N coins on a board with N rows and N columns such that every column contains exactly one coin? (CSIR-NET-JUN-2017)

a) N   **b) N(N-1)(N-2)....2x1**   c) N^2 d) N^N

Hint:
Let the value of N is 3 .
The number of possibility = 3! = 3 x 2 x 1 = 3 (3 – 1) x (3 -2)
For value N it will be =N! = N x (N-1) x (N – 2)…….

9. The number of three English words, having at least one consonant, but not having two consecutive constants, is   (CSIR-NET-DEC-2017)

a) 2205   **b) 3780**   c) 2730   d) 3360

Hint:

 There are 21 consonant and 5 vowels in English letter.

C	V	V	21 X 5 X 5	= 525
V	C	V	5 X 21 X 5	=525
V	V	C	5 X 5 X 21	=525
C	V	C	21 X 5 X 21	=2205
				3780

10. In how many distinguishable ways can the letters of the word CHANCE be arranged? (CSIR-NET-DEC-2016)

a) 120   b) 720   **c) 360**   d) 240

Hint:

CHANCE HAS 6 DIGITS AND C TWO TIMES REAPETING DIGIT. THER FORE 6! /2!
=720/2 = 360

11. **Secondary colours are made by a mixture of three primary colours: Red, Green and Blue in different proportions; each of the primary colours comes in 8 possible levels. Grey corresponds to equal proportions of Red, Green and Blue. How many of grey exist in this scheme? (CSIR-NET -DEC-2015)**

a)8^3 **b) 8** c) 3^8 d)8x3

Hint:

R1 R2 R3 R4 R5 R6 R7 R8

G1 G2 G3 G4 G5 G6 G7 G8

B1 B2 B3 B4 B5 B6 B7 B8

GR1 GR2 GR3 GR4 GR5 GR6 GR7 GR8

12. A code consists of at most two identical letters followed by at most four identical digits. The code must have at least one letter and one digit. How many distinct codes can be generated using letters A to Z and digits 1 to 9? (CSIR-NET-DEC-2014)

a) 936 b) 1148 **c) 1872** d) 2574

Hint:

As the code must have at least one letter and one digit and there should be at most 2 identical letters followed by at most four identical digits then the possibility of codes must be 8.
LD , LDD,LDDD,LDDDD ; LLD , LLDD, LLDDD ; LLDDDD --→ 8 possibility
AA, BB, ………., ZZ AND   1111,2222,……….,9999(Here We have 26 alphabets and number 9).
So, distinct codes can be generated using letters A to Z and digits 1 to 9 = 26 x 9 x 8 =26 x 72 =1872

13. Suppose in a box there are 20 red, 30 black, 40 blue and 50 white balls. What is the minimum number of balls to be drawn, without replacement, so that you are certain about getting 4 red, 5 black, 6 blue and 7 white balls? (CSIR-NET-JUN-2014)

a) 140 **b) 97** c) 104 d) 124

Hint:

The worst case is that only after taking all the Red, Black and Blue balls, we get first White ball. So, in total 20+30+40=90 balls before the first White ball is drawn. Now only White balls are remaining .Hence, the next seven balls to come can only be white balls, making the total count 97.

14. 366 players participate in a knock-out tournament. In each round all competing players pair together and play a match, the winner of each match moving to the next round. If at the end of a round there are an odd number of winners, the unpaired one move to the next round without playing a match. What is the total number of matches played? (CSIR-NET-DEC-2013)

a) 366　　　　　b) 282　　　　　**c) 365**　　　　　d) 418

Let us example of 6 players,

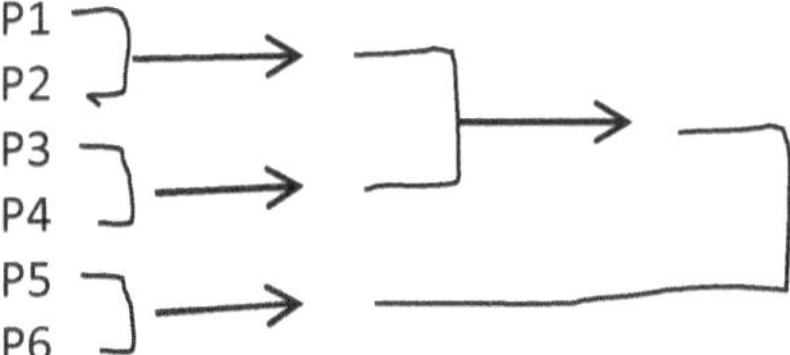

If there is six players then the number of match played will be 5 i.e. 6 – 1 =5
and therefore
If there is 366 players then the number of match played will be 365 i.e. 366 – 1 =365

15. How many 9 digit positive integers are there, the sum of squares of whose digits is 2? (CSIR-NET-DEC-2013)

a) 8　　　　　b) 9　　　　　c) 10　　　　　d) 11

Hint:

The only possibility when the sum of the squares of the digits will be 2 if the number contains two "1". In this case, the 1st digit should be 1, and any one of the remaining 8 digits should be 1. All the other entries should be 0.For example, 100000001 is a nine digit number, whose sum of squares of digits is 2. Since, 1st digit is fixed and the other 1 can occupy any of the 8 positions, there can be 8 such numbers.

16. During a summer vacation, of 20 friends from a hostel, each wrote a letter to each of all others. The total number of letters written was (CSIR-NET-JUN-2013)

a) 20   b) 400   c) 200   **d) 380**

Hint:

20 persons, each wrote a letter to every other person.Therefor each person send 19 letters. So the total number of letters will be 20 X 19 =380

17. Suppose there are socks of N different colours in a box. If you take out one sock at a time , what is the maximum number of socks that you have to take out before a matching pair is found? Assume that N is an even number. (CSIR-NET-DEC-2012)

a) N   b) N+1   c) N-1   d) N/2

Hint:

For the case of N socks we get a matching pair after N takes by considering the worst case that can happen for the given case.

18. What is the number of distinct arrangements of the letters of the word UGCCSIR so that U and I cannot come together? (CSIR-NET-DEC-2012)

a) 2520   b) 720   c) 1520   **d) 1800**

Total arrangement = 7! / 2! , Let assume In 7th option UI come together then (UI) GCCSR = 6! / 2! x 2 (as UI & IU)
The number of distinct arrangements of the letters of the word UGCCSIR so that U and I cannot come together is 7! / 2!   -   6! / 2! x 2 = (6! x 7)/2 − 6! = 6! (7/2 -1) =720 x 5/2 =1800

<u>NUMBER SYSTEM</u>

1. Find the value of f (0) if f(x+2) = $(x+1)^{34}$ – $(x+1)^{33}$ + 5. (CSIR-NET-NOV-2020)

a) 5   **b) 7**   c) 6   d) 72

Hint:
Let x= -2 and putting the value of x in f(x+2) = $(x + 1)^{34}$ – $(x + 1)^{33}$ + 5, we get f (-2+2) = $(-2 + 1)^{34}$ – $(-2 + 1)^{33}$ + 5
Or, f (0) = $(- 1)^{34}$ – $(- 1)^{33}$ + 5 = 1 – (-1) +5 = 1 + 1+ 5=7

2. Two varieties A and B of rice cost Rs.30 and Rs.90 per kg whereas two varieties C and D of pulses, Rs.100 and Rs.120 per kg, respectively.

If at least one kg each of A and B and at least half a kg each of C and D have to be purchased, then the minimum and maximum costs of a total of 5 kg of these provision are, respectively ?(CSIR-NET-DEC-2019)
a) Rs.150 and Rs.600   b) Rs.260 and Rs.530 c) **Rs.290 and Rs.470** d) Rs.370 and Rs.460

Hint.

A		B		C		D		Total	
1 kg	Rs.30	1 kg	Rs.90	½ kg	Rs.50	½ kg	Rs.60	3 kg	Rs.230
2 kg	Rs.60							5 kg	Rs.290

For minimum cost we have to purchase more of that product which has fewer prices.

A		B		C		D		Total	
1 kg	Rs.30	1 kg	Rs.90	½ kg	Rs.50	½ kg	Rs.60	3 kg	Rs.230
						2 kg	Rs.240	5 kg	Rs.470

For maximum cost we have to purchase more of that product which has higher price.

3. The difference, the sum and the product of two integers are in the proportion 1: 3: 10. The two Integers are? (CSIR-NET-DEC-2019)

     a) 3, 9   b) 2, 5   **c) 5, 10**   d) 3, 10

Hint:

Let the two integers are x and y . Therefore $(x - y) : (x + y) : xy = 1 : 3 : 10$ or, $(x - y) : (x + y) : xy = 1k : 3k : 10k$ (k is the common factor) Now $(x - y) + (x + y) = 1k + 3k$ or, $2x = 4k$ or, $x = 2k$, Similarly , $(x - y) - (x + y) = 1k - 3k$ or, $-2y = -2k$ or, $y = k$. Now $xy = (2k)*(k)$ and this should be $= 10k$, or, $2k = 10$ or, $k = 5$. Therefore, $x = 2k$, $2*5 = 10$ and $y = k = 5$

4. The difference between the squares of two consecutive integers is 408235. The sum of the number is?(CSIR-NET-DEC-2019)

a.16324   b.27061   c.180235

d.408235

Hint: -

Let the two consecutive integers are x and y. As per questions $x^2 - y^2$ =408235,.

Again, we know that the difference between two consecutive integers is always 1. So, x- y =1.

Now, we have x^2 y^2 =408235 i.e. (x ı y) (x   y)=408235 i.e. x ı y = 408235 as x − y =1.

So the correct answer is d.408235

5. Given that K! =1x2x3x……..x k, which is the largest among the following numbers? (CSIR-NET-DEC-2019)

A $(2!)^{1/2}$

B $(3!)^{1/3}$

C $(4!)^{1/4}$

D $\dfrac{(3!)}{2}$

Ans. D

Hint:

K! --- We have to understand what factorial is. So, 4!= 1x2x3x4 ,similarly 3! = 1x2x3

Now, $(2!)^{1/2}$= $(1 \times 2)^{1/2}$=$(2)^{1/2}$=1.41, $(3!)^{1/3}$ $= (6)^{1/3} < (2^3)^{1/3}$,$(4!)^{1/4}$=$(24)^{1/4}$ >$(2^4)^{1/4}$, $(3^4)^{1/4}$ >$(24)^{1/4}$ >$(2^4)^{1/4}$,

, $3 > (24)^{1/4} > 2$,(3!)/2=6/2=3

6. Which of the following 7-digit numbers cannot be perfect square?(CSIR-NET-DEC-2019)

A=45xyz26   B=2xyz175   C=xyz3310

a) Only A   b) Only B   c) Only C   **d) All Three**

Hint:

$1^2=1$
$2^2=4$
$3^2=9$
$4^2=16$
$5^2=25$
$6^2 =36$
$7^2 = 49$
$8^2=64$
$9^2 = 81$
$10^2=100$

In case of A=45xyz26   , if it is a square then the unit position digit should be one of the 1, 4, 5,6,9,0. As the last digit are 6, so there is a possibility that A may be a perfect square. In above example $4^2=16$ & $6^2 =36$,that means ,if A is a perfect square then the tenth position digit should be odd number(odd number 1,3,5,7,9…) but in A tenth position digit is even (even number 2). So A cannot be a perfect square.($4^2=16$,$6^2 =36$,$16^2=256$, $24^2=576$ ……….. unit digit =6 and tenth position digit will be odd)

In case of B=2xyz175, if it is a square then the unit position digit should be one of the 1, 4, 5,6,9,0. As the unit digit is 5, so there is a possibility that B may be a perfect square. In above example $5^2=25$, that means, if B is a perfect square then the tenth position digit should be even number (even number 2, 4,6,8…..) , but in B tenth position digit is odd number. So, B cannot be a perfect square.

In case of C=xyz3310, if it is a square then the unit position digit should be one of the *1, 4, 5*,6,9,0. As the unit digit is 0, so there is a possibility that C may be a perfect square. In above example $10^2=100$, that means, if C is a perfect square then the tenth position digit should also be 0 ($10^2=100$, $20^2=400$,$30^2=900$,…..) , but in C tenth position digit is not zero. So, C cannot be a perfect square. So, no one of A, B&C is a perfect square. Hence the correct answer should be d) All Three

7. Which of the following is the largest? (CSIR-NET-JUN-2019)

A 2^{50}

B 3^{40}

C 4^{30}

D 5^{20}

Ans.B

Hint:

$2^{50}= (2^5)^{10}=(32)^{10}\ 3^{40}=(3^4)^{10}=(81)^{10}\ 4^{30}=(4^3)^{10}=(64)^{10}\ 5^{20}=(5^2)^{10}=(25)^{10}$

8. The value of a physical quantity is measured to be 3.4587 ($\overset{+}{-}$) 0.0022. Which one of the following is the appropriate representation of the result taking the errors in account?(CSIR-NET-JUN-2019)

a) 3.4567   b) 3.457   **c) 3.46**   d) 3.5

Hint:
3.4587 + 0.0022=3.4609 = 3.46   and   3.4587 -0.0022=3.4565 = 3.456=
3.46

9. In a city, each person has at least one hair on his / her head. At least two persons in this city are guaranteed to have exactly the same number of hair on their heads if the population of the city?
(CSIR-NET-JUN-2019)

   a) **Is greater than the maximum possible number of hair on the head.**
   b) Is less than the maximum possible number of hair on the head.
   c) Has at least one pair of identical twins.
   d) Is generally homogeneous.

Hint:
For a guaranteed two people having same number of hair on their head,
the population has to be greater than the maximum possible number.

10.Which of the following number is a prime numbers? (CSIR-NET-JUN-2019)

a) 183   b) 121   **c) 157**   d) 10201

Hint:

a) 183 = 61 x 3   b) 121= 11 x 11   c) 157   d) 101 x 101. So correct answer is c).

11. The number of digits you have to type to write all the page numbers of a book starting from 1(first page) is 2019. What is the number of pages in the book?(CSIR-NET-JUN-2019)

a) 609   b) 610   **c) 709**   d) 710

Hint:
1 -9 = 9 pages & 9 digits, 10 - 99 = 90 pages & 90 x 2 = 180 digits, 100 – 999 =900pages & 900 x 3 = 2700 digits, as there is only 2019 digits, so we may write =100 - y = 3 y digits. Now, 9 +180+3y=2019 or, 3y = 2019 – 189 =1830 or, y = 610pages
Then total pages = 9 +90 +610 =709 pages.

[Page RangePages Digits
    0-9   9 x 1 =9
    10-99   90 x 2 = 180
 100-999   610 x3 =1830 (2019-9-180=1830, 1830/3=610)
 Therefore Total pages = 9+ 90 + 610 =709]

12.Marks (out of 30) of seven students in an examination are 4,15,6,7,5,a and b where a(>0) is a multiple of 4 and b is a prime . What is the maximum possible value of the difference between the maximum and minimum marks? (CSIR-NET-DEC-2018)

a) 25   **b) 26**   c)27   d)29

Hint:

Here given that a is multiple of 4 , so maximum value of a should be 28 (as Marks is out of 30). Here also given that b is a prime. The first prime numbers are 2, 3, 5,7,11,13,17,19.23 and 29. So, the minimum value of b should be 2. Now all the numbers are 4, 15, 6, 7,5,28 and 2. The difference between maximum and minimum number=28 – 2 =26

13. At a Birthday party, every child gets 2 chocolates, every mother gets 1 chocolate, while no father gets a chocolate. In total 69 persons get 70 chocolates. If the number of children is half of the number of

mothers and fathers together, then how many fathers are there? (CSIR-NET-DEC-2018)

a) 22   b) 26   c) 27   d) 29

Hint:
Let Child = C, Mother =M and Father =F
Given: 2C + 1 M =70   , C+M+F = 69 and C=1/2 *(M+F) or 2C= M + F

From C+M+F = 69 , by putting value of M + F , we get C + 2C = 69 or, 3C = 69 or, C =23
Now from 2C + 1M =70 we get 2 *23 +M=70 or, M=70-46 = 24 ,
therefore as C+M+F =69 , So putting the value of C and F we get F=69-M-C=69-24-23=22

14.If D= ABC + BCA + CAB where A,B and C are decimal digits, then D is divisible by : **(CSIR-NET-DEC-2018)**
 a) 37 and 29   **b) 37 but not 29**   c)29 but not 37   d) neither 29 nor 37

Hint:
D= (100A +10B +C) + (100B+10C+A) + (100C+10A+B)
=111A+111B+111C= 111(A+B+C). This means that D is always multiple of 111 and we know that 111 is divisible by 37 but not by 29. (37 * 3 = 111)

14. In an examination, 100 questions of 1 mark each are given. After the examination, 20 questions are deleted from evaluation, leaving 80 questions with a total of 100 marks. Students A had answered 4 of the deleted questions correctly and got 40 marks, whereas student B had answered 10 of the deleted questions correctly and get 35 marks. In these situations: (CSIR-NET-DEC-2018)

a) A and B were equally benefited b) A and B lost equally **c) B lost more than A** d) A lost more than B

100 questions have 100 marks, therefore, for each questions has 1 mark. After deletion of 20 questions, 80 questions have 100 marks and therefore each question have 1.25 marks (100/80). As deleted questions have no marks, so, one who has answered more deleted questions he gets less marks. Now, in

question correct answer will be c) as A had answered 4 deleted questions and B had answered 10 deleted questions.

15. Two solutions X and Y containing ingredients A, B and C in proportions a:b:c and c:b:a ,respectively are mixed for the resultant mixture to have A, B and C in equal proportions, it is necessary that :   (CSIR-NET-DEC-2018)

a) b=(c – a)/2   b) c=(a + b)/2   c) c = (a - b)/2   **d) b= (c + a)/2**

Hint:

Let the common factor of the proportions are k , then X= ak : bk : ck and Y=ck : bk : ak . Now in the mixtures of X and Y, the ingredients will be (a + c)k : 2bk : (c + a)k. Since they are in equal proportions in the mixture, we have 2bk= (a + c)k, Therefore, 2b = (a + c) or, b = (a + c)/2

16. Consider a number 54 expressed in a base different from ten. What is the base of this number system if its equivalent value in the decimal system is 49? (CSIR-NET-DEC-2018)

a) 1   b) 3   c) 6   **d) 9**

Hint:

Analyse all options:
Option: a) 5 x 1 +4 =9 (it is not equal to 49)
Option: b) 5 x 3 +4 =19 (it is not equal to 49)
Option: c) 5 x 6 +4 =34 (it is not equal to 49)
Option: a) 5 x 9 + 4 =49 (it is equal to 49)

17. Mohan lent Geeta as much money as she already had. She then spent Rs.10. Next day, he again lent as much money as Geeta now had, and she spent Rs.10 again. On the third day, Mohan again lent as much money as Geeta now had, and she again spent Rs.10. If Geeta was left with no money, at the end of the third day, how much money did she have initially? (CSIR-NET-DEC-2018)

a) Rs.11.25   b) Rs.10   c) Rs.1.75   **d) Rs.8.75**

Hint: Let Mohan Lent Rs.x to Geeta, then

Day	Mohan	Geeta	Geeta have after spent
1 st	x	x + x=2x	2x - 10
2 nd	2x-10	(2x – 10) + (2x – 10)=4x-20	4x-20-10=4x-30

3 rd	4x -30	4x-30+4x-30=8x-60	8x-60-10=8x-70

As per question, $8x - 70 = 0$ or, $8x = 70$ or, $x = 70/8 = 8.75$

18. Nine-eleventh of the members of a parliamentary committee is men. Of the men, two-thirds are from the Rajya Sabha. Further, 7/11 of the total committee members are from Rajya Sabha. What fraction of the total number are women from the Lok Sabha? (CSIR-NET-JUN-2018)

(A) 1/11   (B) 6/11   (C) 2/11   (D) 3/11

Hint:

	RS	LS	TOT
MEN	2/3 * 9/11= 6/11	(9/11 - 6/11)= 3/11	9/11
WOMEN	1/11	1/11	2/11
TOT	7/11	4/11	11/11

19. How much gold and copper (in g), respectively, are required to make a 120 g bar of 22 carat gold? (CSIR-NET-JUN-2018)

a) 90 and 30   b) 100 and 20   **c) 110 and 10**   d) 120 and 0

In 22 carat gold, there are 22 g gold and 2 g copper, therefore, in 120g bar, there will be Copper= (2/24)*120=120/12=10 and gold will be= (22/24)*120 = 110, so the Correct option will be c) 110 g and 10 g

20. What is the last digit of $(2017)^{2017}$ (CSIR-NET-JUN-2018)

a) 1   b) 3   **c) 7**   d) 9

Hint:
Last Digit
$7^1 = 7$
$7^2 = 9$
$7^3 = 3$
$7^4 = 1$

$7^5 = 7$
$7^6 = 9$
$7^7 = 3$
$7^8 = 1$

So, we have to divide the power by cycle 4. i.e.2017 / 4 = 504   & reminder 1 , so the last digit will be 7 as the last digit of 7^1 is 7, similarly if reminder is 2 then last digit will be 9 and so on. To prove it, take the example of 7^5 =16807, here the last digit is 7.

21. In a 100 m race A beats B by 10 m. B beats C by 5 m. By how many meters does A beats C? (CSIR-NET-JUN-2018)

(A) 15.0 m　　　　(B) 5.5 m　　　　(C) 10.5 m　　　　**(D) 14.5 m**

Hint:

When A travels → 100m ,then B travels 90 m .Again when B travels 100m then C travels 95: therefore when b travels 90 m then C travels (95/100)*90=85.5m , So, A beats C by 100-85.5=14.5 m

22. A fuel station sold diesel costing Rs. 15000 to 150 persons on a day. If the lower limit of sale to a person is Rs. 50, what is the maximum amount in rupees for which one person could have purchased diesel on that day? (CSIR-NET-JUN-2018)

a) 7450　　　　b) 7500　　　　**c) 7550**　　　　d) 7600

Hint:

		Persons	Amount spent
Lower Limit	Rs.50	149	7450
Maximum Amt.		1	7550
		150	15000

23. A long distance runner finds a water station after completing 1/7th of the total distance. After covering another 1/6 th of the total distance he gets medical-aid station. Another runner joins him 4 km after the medical aid station. The second runner stops 4 km before the

completion of run, covering ½ of the total distance. What is the total distance? (CSIR-NET-JUN-2018)

a) 21 km   b) 30 km   c) 42 **km**   d) 50 km

Hint:

Let x is the total distance.

x/7 +x/6 + 4 + x/2 +4 =x or, x-x/7-x/6-x/2 = 8 or, 42x-6x-7x-21x =8 * 42 or, 8x =8 *42 or, x=42

24. The sum of two numbers is equal to sum of square of 11 and cube of 9. The larger number is $(5)^2$ less than square of 25. What is the value of the sum of twice of 24 percent of the smaller number and half of the larger number? (CSIR-NET-DEC-2017)

a) 415   b) 400   c) 410   **d) 420**

Hint:

Let x and y are the two numbers. Then as per questions, $x + y = (11)^2 + (9)^3 = 121 + 729 = 850$ and $x = (25)^2 - (5)^2 = 625 - 25 = 600$, Therefore larger number is 600 and smaller number is = 850-600=250,

Now 2*(24/100)*250 + ½ *600 =48*250/100+300 =120+300=420

25. A, B & C are three distinct digits. If they are added as below

```
  A       B       C
+ A       B       C
+ A       B       C
  C       C       C
```
Find out the value of A, B & C. (CSIR-NET-JUN-2017)

a) A=3 B=4   C= 5   b) A=2 B=3   C=1 c) A=5 B=1   C= 3 **d) A=1 B=8   C= 5**

Hint: Put the value of A, B & C in the above chart from answer options. In case of option a) 3 4 5 +3 4 5 + 3 4 5 =1035 but it should be 555, so, it is wrong answer. In case of option b) & c) the value of C is 1 & 3.

Therefore after adding it should be 111 &333 but it is not possible. In case of option d) 185+185+185=555 which is correct option.

26. **4. If P+$^1/_Q$=1 and Q+$^1/_R$=1 then what is PQR?** (CSIR-NET-JUN-2017)

a)-1   b) 2   c) -2   d) cannot be calculated

Hint:

P+$^1/_Q$=1   i.e. PQ+1=Q i.e.   PQR +R=RQ (Multiply R with both sides)
i.e PQR = RQ-R ------- (i)
Again, Q+$^1/_R$=1 i.e. QR+1 = R i.e RQ = R – 1 , Now we are putting the value of RQ in equation (i), so PQR= (R-1)-R i.e PQR = -1 , So the correct answer is **a)-1**

27. N is a two-digit number such that the product of its digits when added to their sum equals N. The unit digit of N would be?(CSIR-NET-JUN-2017)

a)1   b)7   c)8   **d)9**

Hint: let x y is the product and their sum is x + y of the two digits x and y , as per questions , x +y +xy =N and N=10x + y ,Therefore , x + y + xy =10x +y or, y + xy-y=10x-x or, xy = 9x or, y=9

28. Which the odd one is out based on a divisibility test? 154, 286, 363, 474,572, 682. (CSIR-NET-JUN-2017)

a) 474   b) 572   c) 682   d) 154

Hint:
The divisibility of 11 is the difference between the sum of odd position digits and sum of the even position digits must be 0. Now 474 = (4+4)-7 which is not 0; 572= (5+2)-7=0 , 682=(6+2)-8=0, 154=(1+5)-4=0

29. If the product of 3 consecutive positive integers is equal to their sum, then what would be the sum of their squares? (CSIR-NET-JUN-2017)

a) 9   **b) 14**   c) 16   d) 24

Hint:

Let 1, 2 , 3 are the 3 consecutive positive integers. Product= 1 x2 x3 = 6 and Sum = 1 + 2 + 3 =6

Therefore, $1^2 + 2^2 + 3^2 = 1 + 4 + 9 = 14$, so, correct answer is b). [let the 3 consecutive positive integers are (x-1), x, (x+1). As per question (x-1). x .(x+1) = (x-1) + x + (x+1)=3x Or, $(x^2-1) . x = 3x$ or, $(x^2-1) . x -3x = 0$ or, $x(x^2-1- 3) = 0$ or $x(x^2-4) = 0$ but x≠0, so ,$x^2-4 = 0$, so x = 2, the three consecutive no aro (2 1) , 2 ,(2 +1) i.c. 1 ,2 , 3].

30. Choose the four- digit number, in which the product of the first and fourth digits is 40 and the product of the middle digits is 28. The thousands digit is as much less as the unit digit as the hundreds digit is less than the tens digit:

a) **5478**   b) 5748   c) 8745   d) 8475

Hint: Let the Number is   1000x+100y+10z+k. Now as per questions, xk = 40 and yz=28 and k-x = z-y

 By taking options, we get option a) satisfies all the conditions and other options are not satisfying.

31. N is a four-digit number. If the leftmost digit is removed, resulting three-digit number is 1/9th of N. How many such N is possible? (CSIR-NET-JUN-2016)

       a)10   b) 9   c) 8   **d) 7**

Hint:

Let N = abcd   be the four-digit number. Given 1/9 * N =bcd-----(1)
Put according to place value in above (1) ,   1/9(1000a+100b+10c+d) =100b+10c+d or, 1000a+100b+10c+d=900b+90c+9d or, 1000a = 800b+80c+8d or, 125a= 100b+10c+d , Therefore , 125a = bcd

a	bcd	N=abcd
1	125	1125
2	250	2250
3	375	3375
4	500	4500

5	625	5625
6	750	6750
7	875	7875
8	1000	Not accessible

So, there is total 7 numbers.

32. Binomial theorem in algebra gives $(1 + x)^n = a_0 + a_1x+a_2x^2 + ... + a_nx^n$, where $a_0, a_1, ...,a_n$ are constants depending on n. What is the sum of $a_0+a_1+a_2+.....+a_n$? (CSIR-NET-DEC-2014)

a) 2^n   b) n   c) n^2 d) n^2+n

Hint:

Let x = 1 , then $(1 + x)^n = a_0 + a_1x+a_2x^2 + ... + a_nx^n$ will be $(1 + 1)^n = a_0 + a_1+a_2^2 + ... + a_n$and therefore
$2^n = = a_0 + a_1+a_2^2 + ... + a_n$

33. The least significant bit of an 8-bit binary number is zero. A binary number whose value is 8 times the previous number has? (CSIR-NET-DEC-2014)

a) 12 bits ending with three zeros   **b) 11 bits ending with four zeros**
c) 11 bits ending with three zeros   d) 12 bits ending with four zeros

Hint:

Least significant bit is the last bit of a binary number. Let us take a typical 8-bit binary number, for example 10000010. Now, the least significant bit here is zero. We have to determine the binary number whose value is 8 times the above number.

Note: rules of binary number whose value is 8 times the above number.

Note: rule of binary addition: 0 + 0 =0 , 1 + 1 =10, 10+10=100, 100+100=1000, 1000+1000=10000

Note: In any number system, for any number x, x + x =2x, 2x+2x=4x , 4x+4x=8x, i.e 8 times the number x.

So, to find 8 times the number 10000010, we should perform 3 cycles of the above-mentioned binary addition.

2 times: 10000010 + 10000010 = 100000100, 4 times : 100000100 + 100000100 = 1000001000
8 times: 1000001000 + 1000001000=10000010000, Therefore, 11 bits ending with four zeros.

34. If n is a positive integer, then n(n+1)(n+2)(n+3)(n +4)(n+5)(n+6) is divisible by (CSIR-NET-DEC-2014)

a) 3 but not 7   **b) 3 and 7**   c) 7 but not 3   d) neither 3 nor 7

Hint:

It is fact that in every three consecutive integers, there should be a multiple of 3 and in every seven consecutive integers, there should be a multiple of 7. Now, n, n+1 ...., n+6 are 7 consecutive numbers. So, there will be a multiple of 3 and 7 in these numbers. Therefore, n (n+1)(n+2)(n+3)(n+4)(n+5)(n+6), having consecutive integers is divisible by 3 and 7.

35.If N, E&T are distinct positive integers such that NxExT=2013, then which of the following is the maximum possible sum of N, E&T? (CSIR-NET-DEC-2014)

a) 39   b) 2015   **c) 675**   d) 671

Hint:
NxExT=2013 i.e. NxExT=671 x 3   i.e. NxExT=671 x 3 x 1 , So N=671   E=3   T= 1, therefore N+E+T = 671+3+1=675. So, the correct answer is c) 675.

36. The sum of first n natural numbers with one of them missed is 42. What is the number that was missed? (CSIR-NET-DEC-2014)

a) 1   b) 2   **c) 3**   d) 4

Hint:
1+2+3+4+5+6+7+8+9 = 45, 45-42=3

37. a mouse has to go from a point a to B without retracing any part of the path and never moving backwards. What is the total number of distinct paths that the mouse may take to go from A to B? (CSIR-NET-DEC-2014)

a) 11   **b) 48**   c) 72   d) 24

Path 2 x 4 x3 x 2 =48

38. We define a function f(N) = sum of digits of N, expressed as a decimal number (CSIR-NET-DEC-2014)

E.g. f(137) =1 +3 +7=11
Evaluate $f(2^7 3^5 5^6)$.

a)10   **b)18**   c)28   d)11
Hint:
$(2^7 3^5 5^6) = 2 \times 3^5 \times 2^6 \times 5^6 = 2 \times 3^5 \times (2 \times 5)^6 = 2 \times 3^5 \times 10^6 = 2 \times 243 \times 10^6$
$=486 \times 10^6 = 486000000.$
Thus, $(2^7 3^5 5^6)$ = sum of digits of 486000000=4 + 8 + 6 + 0 =18

39. The equation $m^2 - 33n + 1 = 0$, where m & n are integers has? (CSIR-NET-DEC-2014)

a) no solution   b) exactly one solution   c) exactly two solutions
d) Infinitely many solutions

Hint:
Given $m^2 - 33n +1 = 0$, $m^2 = 33n - 1$, m = v(33n-1) [root over (33n-1)]
There is no such integer 'n' which satisfies the equation. Hence, there is no solution to the given equation.

40. Which of the following Number is perfect Square? (CSIR-NET-DEC-2014)

a) 1022121   b) 2042122   c) 3063126   d) 4083128

Hint:

We know that a perfect square does not end with 2, 3, 7 or 8. Thus, we can say that (2) and (4) cannot be the correct options. Doing the prime factorization of options (1) and (3). 3063126 = 2 x 3 x 11 x 46411, in which the factors 2, 3, 11, 46411 all have multiplicities 1, which is odd. Thus, 3063126 should not be a perfect square. 1022121 = 3^2 x 337^2 = $(3 \times 337)^2$, which is clearly a perfect square.

41. Suppose n is a positive integer. Then $(n^2+n)(2n+1)$ (CSIR-NET-JUN-2014)

a) may be not divisible by 2

b) is always divisible by 2 but may not be divisible by 3

c) is always divisible by 3 but may not be divisible by 6

d) is always divisible by 6

Hint:

Let n =1 then $(n^2+n)(2n+1)=6$, if n=2 then $(n^2+n)(2n+1)=30$, if n=3 then $(n^2+n)(2n+1)=84$, So, **$(n^2+n)(2n+1)$** is always divisible by 2,3,6 ,so the correct answer is d) [12 +22 +32 +……+ n2 = n(n+1)(2n + 1)/6 = $(n^2+n)(2n+1)$/ 6]

42. Consider the set of numbers $\{17^1, 17^2, ….., 17^{300}\}$.How many of these numbers end with the digit 3 ? (CSIR-NET-JUN-2014)

a) 60   **b) 75**   c) 100   d) 150

Hint:

17^1 = 7
17^2 = 9
17^3= 3
17^4 = 1
17^5 = 7
17^6 = 9
17^7 = 3
17^8 = 1

Last digit will be 3 on one of the every four number. So   300/4=75

43. 6. If AxB = 24, BxC=32 and CxD=48 then AxD =? (CSIR-NET-JUN-2014)

a) Cannot be found   **b) is a perfect square**   c) is a perfect cube

d) is odd

Hint:

$(A \times B)(C \times D) = 24 \times 48$ i.e. $(A \times D)(B \times C) = 24 \times 48$ i.e. $A \times D = 24 \times 48 / B \times C = 24 \times 48 / 32 = 36 = (6)^2$

So, the correct answer is b) is a perfect square

44. CSIR-NET-JUNE-2014

Suppose x \y = (x - y)

xoy = (x + y)

x*y = (x × y)

x.y = x × y

+. - and x have their usual meanings.

What is the value of {(197o315)-(197 \315)} (197*315)?

A. 1018   B. 512

C. 2   D. 4   Ans. D

Hint:

Suppose x \y = (x - y)

xoy = (x + y)

x*y = (x × y)

x.y = x × y

+. - and x have their usual meanings

What is the value of {(197o315)-(197 \315)} (197*315)?

A. 1018   B. 512

C. 2   D. 4

45.The following sum is : 1+1-2+3-4+5-6….. -20=? (CSIR-NET-JUN-2014)

a) 10   b) -10   c) -11   **d) -9**

Hint:

1+(1-2)+(3-4)+(5-6)+(7-8)+(9-10)+(11-12)+(13-14)+(15-16)+(17-18)+(19-20)=1-10=-9

46. How many digits are there in 2^{17} x 3^2 x 5^{14} x 7? (CSIR-NET-JUN-2014)

a) 14 b) 15 c) 16 d) 17

Hint:

2^{17} x 3^2 x 5^{14} x 7 = 2^{14} x $2^3 3^2$ x 5^{14} x 7 = (2 x 5)^{14} x 8 x 9 x 7 =(10)^{14} x72 x 7

==(10)^{14} x 504 ; (10)^{14} have 14 digits and 504 have 3 digit = 14 + 3 = 17 digit

47. If a+b+c+d+e = 10 (all positive numbers) , then the maximum value of a x b x c x d x e is ?(CSIR-NET-DEC-2013)

a) 12 b) 32 c) 48 d) 72

Hint:

Maximum of (a,b,c,d,e) is minimum for (2,2,2,2,2). That is a x b x c x d x e =2 x 2 x 2 x 2x 2 = 32

48. For real numbers x and y, x^2 + $(y - 4)^2$ = 0. Then the value of x + y is (CSIR-NET-DEC-2013)

a) 0 b) 2 c) 2 **d) 4**

Hint:

If the sum of square of two numbers is zero, then each number should be equal to zero.

As x^2 + $(y-4)^2$ = 0; Therefore x^2 = 0 and $(y-4)^2$ = 0; x=0 and y=4, x + y = 4

49. (25÷5+3-2x4) + (16x4-3)= ? (CSIR-NET-DEC-2013)

a) **61** b) 22 c) 41/24 d) 1

Hint:

Using BODMAS Rule: (25÷5+3-2x4) + (16x4-3)= ((25 ÷5) +3 – (2 x 4)) +((16 x 4) -3)) = ((5 ÷3) – 8) +((16 x 4) -3 =(8 -8) +(64 – 3) =61

50. Every time a ball falls to ground, it bounces back to half the height it fell from. A ball is dropped from a height of 1024 cm. the maximum height from the ground to which it can rise after the tenth bounce is (CSIR-NET-DEC-2013)

a) 102.4 cm   b) 1.24 cm   **c) 1 cm**   d) 2 cm

Hint:
$1024 \rightarrow 1024(1/2) \rightarrow 1024(1/2)^2 \rightarrow 1024(1/2)^3$ ....$\rightarrow 1024(1/2)^{10}$
Therefore, $1024(1/2)^{10} = 1024(1/1024) = 1$

51. 46. $4^0 + 4^2 + 1/4^2 + 4^{1/2} + 1/4^{1/2}$ equal   (CSIR-NET-DEC-2013)

$4^0 + 4^2 + \dfrac{1}{4^2} + 4^{1/2} + \dfrac{1}{4^{1/2}}$ equals

(a) 4 (b) $4^2 + 4$ (c) $19\dfrac{9}{16}$ (d) $22\dfrac{9}{16}$

Ans. (c)

$4^0 + 4^2 + 1/4^2 + 4^{1/2} + 1/4^{1/2} = 1 + 16 + 1/16 + 2 + 1/2 = 19 + (1/16 + 1/2) = 19 + (9/16)$

52. If a_i, b_i, c_i are distinct, how many terms will the expansion of the product $(a1 + a_2 + a_3)(b_1 + b_2 + b_3 + b_4)(c_1 + c_2 + c_3 + c_4 + c_5)$ contain? (CSIR-NET-DEC-2014)

a) 12   b) 30   c) 23   d) 60

Hint:

$(a1 + a_2 + a_3)(b_1 + b_2 + b_3 + b_4)(c_1 + c_2 + c_3 + c_4 + c_5) \rightarrow (a1 + a_2 + a_3)$ have 3 terms, $(b_1 + b_2 + b_3 + b_4)$ have 4 term and $(c_1 + c_2 + c_3 + c_4 + c_5)$ have 5 terms, So the answer of this question will be 3 x 4 x 5 = 60

$(a+b)(c+d) = ac + ad + bc + bd = 4$ term as $(a+b)$ have 2 term and $(c+d)$ have 2 term.

53. How many pairs of positive integers have GCD 20 and LCM 600? (GCD= greatest common divisor, LCM= least common multiple) (CSIR-NET-JUN-2013)
a)4   b) 0   c) 1   d) 7
Hint:
We know that $\text{GCD}_{(a,b)} \times \text{LCM}_{(a,b)} = a \times b = 20 \times 600 = 1200$
Now, as GCD=20, so there must be two numbers, say 20x and 20y, i.e. a=20x and b= 20y
Therefore, a x b =12000 = (20x)(20y), or, 400xy = 12000, or xy = 30. Now we have to take such option where product of two numbers should be 30.

x	1	2	3	5
y	30	15	10	6

So the correct answer is a) 4.

[20x x 20y =12000, (20 x1) x (20x30) =20 x 600 =12000, (20 x 2) x(20 x15)=40 x 300 =12000 and so on.]

54. CSIR-NET-JUNE-2013

Define $a \otimes b = LCM(a,b) + GCD(a,b)$ and $a \oplus b = a^b + b^a$

What is the value of $(1 \oplus 2) \otimes (3 \oplus 4)$?

Here LCM = least common multiple and GCD = greatest common divisor.

A) 145

B) 286

C) 436

D) 572.

Ans.C

Hint:

$a(+)b = a^b + b^a$, $1 + 2 = 1^2 + 2^1 = 3$, Again $3 + 4 = 3^4 + 4^3 = 81 + 64 = 145$
Now , $(1 + 2) \times (3 + 4) = 3 \times 145$ {a x b
=LCM(a,b)+GCD(a,b)}=LCM(3,145)+GCD(3,145)=3x145+1=425+1=436
145 is not divisible by 3, so , it is co-prime & we know co-prime for LCM is multiplication of the two numbers & GCM will be 1.

55. Choose the largest number. (CSIR-NET-JUN-2013)

a) 2^{500} b) 3^{400} c) 4^{300} d) 5^{200}

Hint:

$2^{500} = 2^{5 \times 100} = (32)^{100}$, $3^{400} = (3)^{4 \times 100} = (81)^{100}$, $4^{300} = (4)^{3 \times 100} = (64)^{100}$, $5^{200} = (5)^{2 \times 100} = (25)^{100}$, so b) is the correct answer.

56. In solving a quadratic equation of the form $x^2+ax+b = 0$, one student took the wrong value of a and got the roots as 6 and 2; while another students took the wrong value of b and got the roots as 6 and 1. What are the correct values of a and b , respectively? (CSIR-NET-JUN-2013)

a) 7 and 12   b) 3 and 4   **c) -7 and 12**   d) 8 and 12

Hint:
If α & β are the roots of the quadratic equation $Ax^2 + Bx + C = 0$ then $\alpha + \beta = -B/A = -a$ and $\alpha\beta = C/A = b$
When one took the wrong value of a then there is correct value of b and the roots are 6 and2, so $\alpha\beta = C/A = b$, 6x2=b i.e., b=12
When one took wrong value of b then there is correct value of a and the roots are6 and 1, so $\alpha + \beta = -B/A = -a$,6+1=-a, or a=-7

57. Suppose you expand the product $(x_1 + y_1)(x_2 + y_2) ......(x_{20} + y_{20})$. How many terms will have only one x and rest y's? (CSIR-NET-JUN-2013)

a) 1   b) 5   c) 10   **d) 20**

Hint:
$(x_1 + y_1)$ ---- 1 term, $(x_1 + y_1) (x_2 + y_2)= (x_1 x_{2 +} x_1 y_2 + x_2 y_1+ y_1 y_2$----------- 2 terms
Continuing like this, we can find that if 20 factors are there in the product, there will be terms in the expression with only 1 x and rest all y's.

58. What is the last digit of $(7)^{73}$ (CSIR-NET-JUN-2013)

a) 1   b) 3   **c) 7**   d) 9
Hint:
Last Digit
$7^1 = 7$
$7^2 = 9$
$7^3 = 3$
$7^4 = 1$
$7^5 = 7$

$7^6 = 9$
$7^7 = 3$
$7^8 = 1$

So, we have to divide the power by cycle 4. i.e.73 / 4 =18 & reminder 1 , so the last digit will be 7 as the last digit of 7^1 is 7, similarly if reminder is 2 then last digit will be 9 and so on. To prove it, take the example of 7^5 =16807, here the last digit is 7.

59. n is a natural number. If n^5 is odd, which of the following is true?

(A) n is odd   (B) n^3 is odd   (C) n^4 is even(CSIR-NET-JUN-2013)

a) A only   b) B only   c) C only   **d) A and B only**

Hint:

Let n=3, so 3^5 = 243 now n =3, n^3 = 27, n4 = 81. Here n is odd, n^3 is odd but n4 is not even, so correct answer is d).

60. Consider the following equation: $x^2 + 4y^2 + 9z^2 = 14x +28y +42z -147$ where x,y and z are real numbers. Then the value of x + 2y +3z is   (CSIR-NET-DEC-2012)

a) 7   b) 14   **c) 21**   d) not unique

Hint:

$x^2 + 4y^2 + 9z^2 = 14x +28y +42z -147$ or, $x^2 - 14x + 4y^2 - 28y + 9z^2 - 42z = -147$
or, $x^2 - 14x + 49 + 4y^2 - 28y +49 + 9z^2 - 42z +49 = -147 +49 +49 +49$
or, $(x - 7)^2 + (2y-7)^2 + (3z-7)^2 = 0$ Therefore, x = 7 , 2y = 7 and 3z =7
or, **x + 2y +3z = 7 + 7 + 7 =21**

61. CSIR-NET-DEC-2012

Which of the following numbers is the largest?

$$2^{3^4}, 2^{4^3}, 3^{4^2}, 4^{2^3}, 4^{3^2}$$

(A) 2^{3^4} (B) 3^{4^2}

(C) 4^{3^2} (D) 4^{2^3}

Ans. A

Hint:

A) 2 to the power 3 to the power 4 = 2 to the power (3x3x3x3)=2to the power $81=2^{81}$

B) 3 to the power 4 to the power 2 = 3 to the power (4x4)=3 to the power $16=3^{16}$ which is less than 4^{16}(Now $4^{16}=(2^2)^{16}=2^{32}$, therefore, $3^{16}< 2^{32}$)

C) 4 to the power 3 to the power 2 = 4 to the power (3x3)=4 to the power $9=4^9=(2^2)^9=2^{18}$

D) 4 to the power 2 to the power 3 = 4 to the power (2x2x2)=4 to the power $8=4^8=(2^2)^8=2^{16}$

62. Which of the following curve just touches the x-axis? (CSIR-NET-DEC-2012)

a) $y= x^2 - x + 1$ b) $y=x^2 -2x +2$ **c) $y=x^2 -10x + 25$** d) $y=x^2-7x+12$

Hint: $x^2 -10x + 25 = 0$ or, $(x - 5)^2 = 0$ or, $x = 5, 5$ which are real and equal roots.

Series

1. If the sum of the next two terms of the series below is x, what is the value of $\log_2 x$? (CSIR-NET-DEC-2012)

 2, -4, 8, -16, 32, -64, 128, ...

    A)   128   B) 10   C) 256   **D) 8**

Hint: $2 \to 2^1 \to -(2)^2 \to 2^3 \to -(2)^4 \to 2^5 \to -(2)^6 \to 2^7 \to -(2)^8 \to 2^9$, Therefore the series will be

2, -4, 8, -16, 32, -64, 128, -256, 512 , So the sum of next two terms x= 512-256=256

Now, $x=256=2^8$, or, $\log_2 x = \log_2 2^8 = 8\log_2 2 = 8$

2. What is the next number of the sequence 24, 30, 33, 39, 51, ….? (CSIR-NET-DEC-2012)

A) 57 B) 69 C) 54 D) 81

Hint: 30-24=6(2+4) , 33 – 30 =3 (3+0) , 39 – 33=6 (3+3) , 51 – 39=12 (3+9) , X – 51= ? (5+1)

Here X=51+6=57 ,{57 – 51=6(5+1)}

3. What is the next number in the "see and tell" sequence? 1, 11, 21, 1211, 111221, ……?(CSIR-NET-DEC-2012)

A) 312211 B) 1112221 C) 1112222 D) 1112131

1 -> One 1 -> 11-> Two One -> 21-> One 2 One 1-> 1211 -> One 1 One 2 two 1-> 111221 -> Three 1 Two 2 One 1 ->1112211

4. (CSIR-NET-DEC-2012)

In a sequence $\{a_n\}$, every term is equal to the sum of all its previous

terms. If $a_1 = 3$, then $\lim \dfrac{a_{n+1}}{a_n}$ is

A) 3 B) 2 C) 1 D) e

Hint: The first term = a_0=3 , So the 2 nd term will also be 3 as every term is equal to the sum of all its previous terms, Therefore, 3 ->3 ->(3+3)=6 ->(3+3+6)=12-> (3+3+6+12)=24 -> (3+3+6+12+24)=48, So the sequence will be 3, 3, 6, 12, 24, 48, ….. Now 48/24=2 , 24/12=2, 12/6=2, 6/3 =2 , so a_{n+1}/a_n=2

5. Find the missing letter? (CSIR-NET-DEC-2012)

Find the missing letter?

A	E G K	C
?		P
U		R
Q		V
B	O J F	D

A) H B) L **C) Z** D) V

Hint:

1	5	7	11	3

- 21 17		16 18 22
2	15 10 6	4

7 – 5= 2;   11-7=4;   18-16=2;   22-18=4;   15-10=5;   10-6=4;   ?-21=5;   21-17=4;

Therefore, ? =5+21=26 =Z

6. The next number of the sequence 1, 5, 14, 30, 55,... is?(CSIR-NET-DEC-2013)

A) 85   B) 90   **C) 91**   D) 95

Hint: 1 + **4** -> 5 + **9** -> 14 + **16** -> 30 + **25** -> 55 + 36 = 91 (**4**=2^2, **9**=3^2, **16**=4^2, **25**=5^2 So, 6^2=36)

7. Consider the sequence of ordered sets of natural numbers :{1},{2,3},{4.5.6},.....What is the last number in the 10th set? (CSIR-NET-DEC-2013)

A) 10   B) 19   **C) 55**   D) 67

Hint: 1st set -> 1(1 digit) , 2nd set -> 2,3 (2 digit), 3rd set -> 4,5,6 (3 digit)-----10th set->(10 digit)
1,2,3,.,10 . Now last number of 2nd set (which is 3) = digit no. of 1st set + digit no. of 2nd set (1 +2->3).
Now last number of 3rd set (which is 6) = digit no. of 1st set +digit no. of 2nd set + digit no. of 3rd set (1+2+3->6).
So, Last no. of 10th set= digit no. of 1st set +digit no. of 2nd set + digit no .of 3rd set +........+ digit no. of 10 set i.e. 1 +2 +3 +4 +5 +6 + 7+ 8+ 9+10= n(n+1)/2= 10(10+1)/2=10*11/2=55

8. What is the next number in the sequence? 39, 42, 46, 50, ...(CSIR-NET-DEC-2013)

A) 52   B) 53   C) 54   **D) 55**

Hint: 42-**39** =**3**   46-42=**4**   50-46=**4**   ? – 50=**5** i.e. 55 – 50 =5

9. A lucky man finds 6 pots of gold coins. He counts the coins in the first four pots to be 60, 30, 20 and 15 respectively. If there is a definite progression, what would be the numbers of coins in the next two pots?(CSIR-NET-JUN-2013)

A)   10 and 5   B) 4 and 2   C) 15 and 15   **D) 12 and 10**

Hint: 30/60 =1/2 , 20/30=2/3 , 15/20 =3/4 So the next two pots ratio will be 4/5 and 5/6
(1/2, 2/3, 3/4, 4/5, 5/6). Let us suppose that the 4th pot have X coins and the 5th Pot have Y coins.
So X/15=4/5 or, X=12 Similarly Y/12=5/6   or, Y=10

10. Find the missing number? (CSIR-NET-JUN-2013)

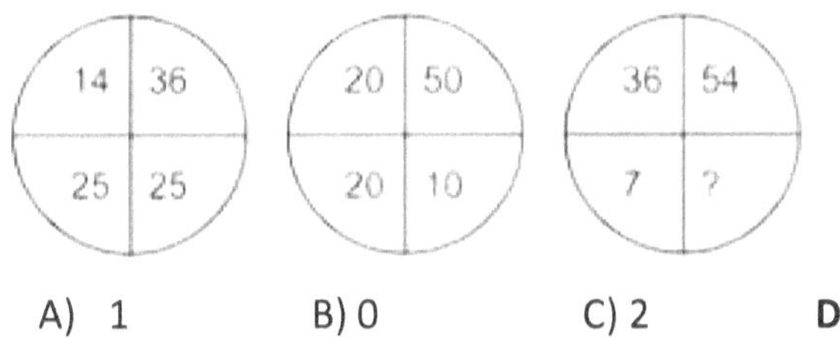

A)   1   B) 0   C) 2   **D) 3**

Hint : 14+36+25+25= 100   20+50+10+20 =100   36+54+?+7=100 or, ?=100-97=3

11. In the Figure, The numbers of circles in the blank rows must be (CSIR-NET-JUN-2013)

A)   12 and 20   B) 13 and 20   **C) 13 and 21**   D) 10 and 11

Hint: 1 , 1 ,2 , 3 , 5 , 8 → 1+1 ->2 ,1+2->3 , 2+3->5 , 3+5->8 , 5+8->13 , 8+13->21

12. Find the missing number in the triangle? (CSIR-NET-JUN-2014)

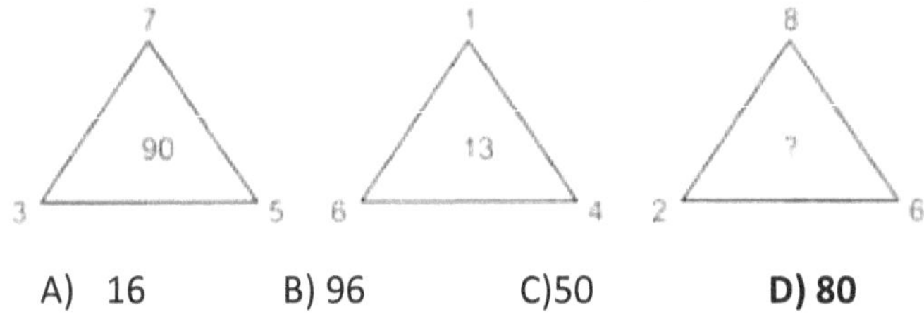

A)   16   B) 96   C)50   **D) 80**

Hint: (3x5x7)-(3+5+7)=90 ; (6x4x1) – (6+4+1)=13 ; (2x6x8)-(2+6+8)= 96-16=80

1**3**. Continue the sequence 2, 5, 10, 17, 28, 41, …, …, …? (CSIR-NET-DEC-2014)

A) 58, 77, 100   B) 64, 81, 100   C) 43, 47, 53   D) 55, 89, 113

Hint:- 2 +3 -> 5 +5 ->10 +7 ->17 + 11 ->28 +13 ->41 +17->58 +19 -> 77 + 23 ->100

We get the next number by adding prime numbers 3,5,7,11,13,17,19,23.

14. What is the next number in the following sequence: 2, 3, 5, 6, 3, 4, 7, 12, 4, 5, 9….(CSIR-NET-JUN-14)

A) 10   **B) 20**   C) 13   D) 6

Hint:- (2, 3, 5, 6), (3, 4, 7, 12),(4, 5, 9, ….).   Now ,   (2, 3, 5, 6) -> 2, 3, (2+3),(2x3) ;

(3, 4, 7, 12) -> 3,4,(3+4),(3x4) ;   (4, 5, 9, ….)-> 4, 5,(4+5),(4x5)   i.e. 4,5,9,20

15. Find the missing number in the sequence? 61, 52, 63, 94, ….. , 18, 001, 121(CSIR-NET-JUN-2014)

A) 46   B) 70   C) 66   D) 44

Hint: 61 (16->4^2) , 52 (25 -5^2), 63(36->6^2),94(49->7^2), (8^2->64->46),......

16. Every month, the price of a particular commodity falls in this order: 1024,640, 400, 250...
What is the next value? (CSIR-NET-DEC-2014)

A) 156.25   B) Approx.39   C) 64   D) 40

Hint: 1024/640=8/5 ; 640/400=8/5; 400/250=8/5; 250/x=8/5 or,
x=250*5/8=156.25

18. What is the next number in the sequence? 2, 3, 4, 7, 6, 11, 8, 15, 10, ...(CSIR-NET-DEC-2014)

A)   12   B) 13   C) 17   **D) 19**

Hint: 2, 4, 6, 8, 10   3, 7, 11, 15, 19

19. Fill in the blank: F2, ... , D8, C16, B32, A64 (CSIR-NET-JUN-2016)

A) C4   **B) E4**   C) C2   D) G16

Hint: 2 ,**4**,8,16,32,64 and F,**E**,D,C,B,A

20. CSIR-NET-JUN-2014

What is the next term in the following sequence?

7, 11, 13, 17, 19, 23, 29.

A) 37   B) 35   C) 31   D) 33

Ans.C

21. CSIR-NET-DEC-2015

The missing number is

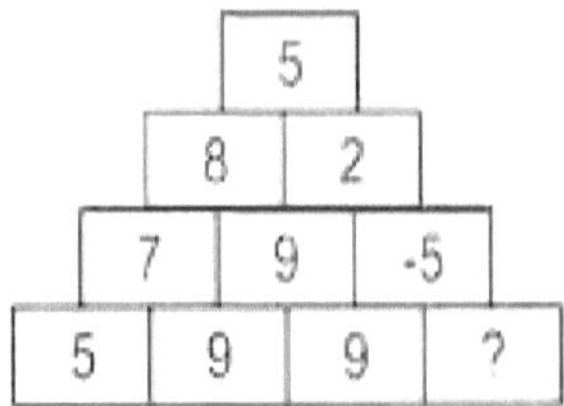

(A) -19 (B) -5 (C) 9 (D) -9

Ans.A

22. What is the value of 1/ 1x2 + 1 / 2x3 + 1/3x4 + …. to ∞?(CSIR-NET-JUN-2013)

A) 2/3 B) 1 C) D) ∞

Hint. $(1/1 – 1/2) + (1/2 – 1/3) + (1/3 – 1/4) + ……..$ to ∞ = 1/1 =1

23. Which of the following options is the best choice for the missing number?(CSIR-NET-JUN-2018)
0.1 , 0.25 , 0.3 , 0.2 , 0.5 , 0.6 , 0.3 , ……………… , 0.9 , 0.4 , 1.0 , 1.2
a) 1.05 b) 0.85 **c) 0.75** d) 0.65

0.1 0.2 0.3 0.4 -- 0.25 0.5 .75 1.0 --- 0.3 0.6 0.9

24. In a sequence of 24 positive integers, the product of any two consecutive integers is 24. If the 17th member of the sequence is 6 then the 7th number is ? (CSIR-NET-JUN-2018)

a) 24 b) 4 **c) 6** d) 17

24=6*4 if 17 is 6 then 15, 13, 11, 9, 7 all have 6.

<u>Non-Verbal Reasoning</u>

1.CSIR-NET-DEC-2018

Find the missing pattern

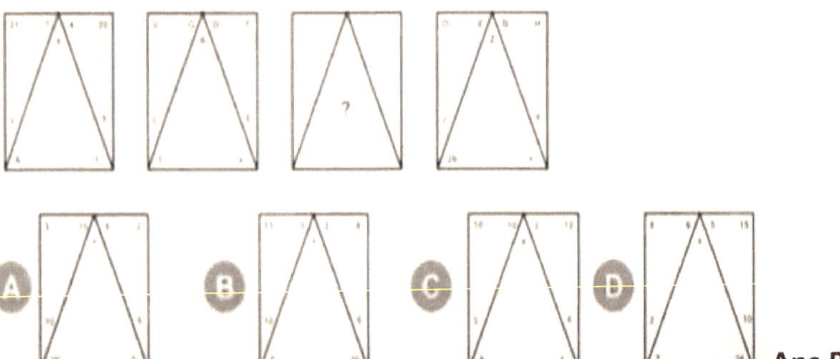

Ans.B

2. CSIR-NET-DEC-2017

Find the missing number

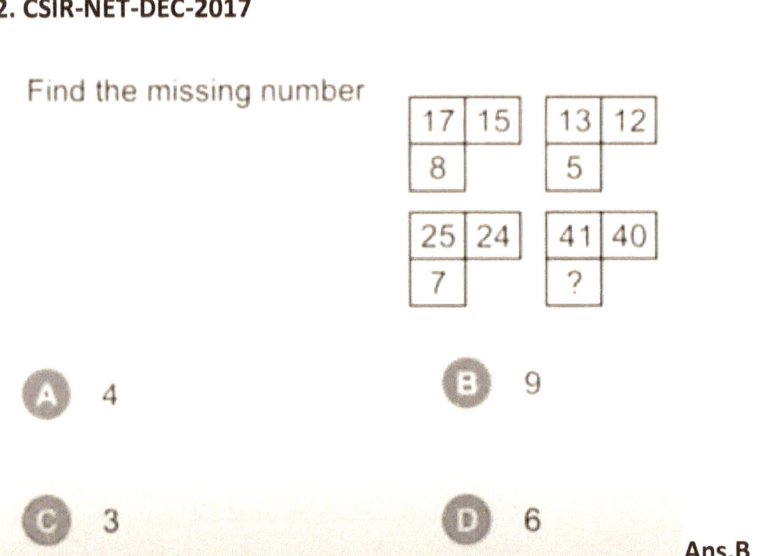

A   4

B   9

C   3

D   6

Ans.B

3. CSIR-NET-DEC-2017

Find he next pattern in the following sequence :

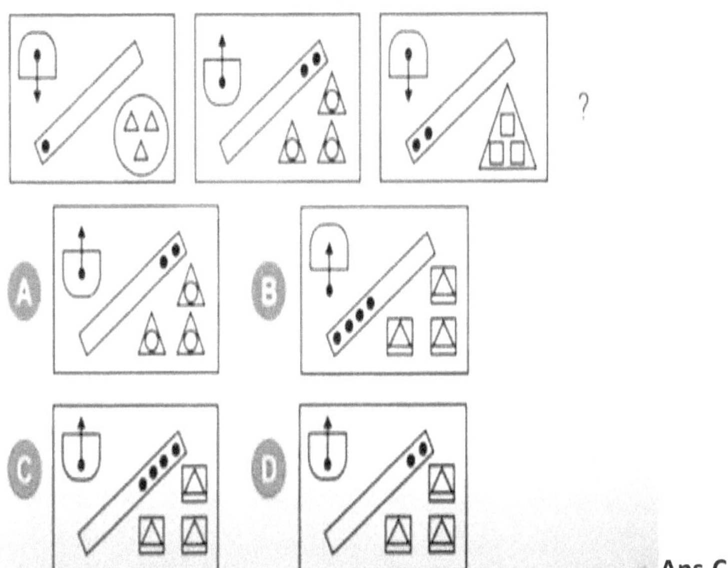

Ans.C

4. CSIR-NET-JUN-2017

If 42 → 26, 71 → 78, 33 → 16 then 62 →

A 68

B 54

C 38

D 39

Ans.C

5. CSIR-NET-JUN-2018

Which should be the correct pattern in the empty square?

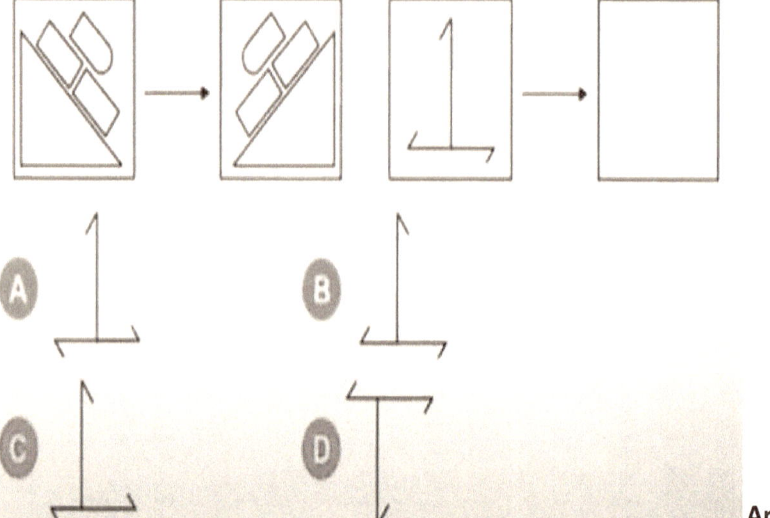

Ans.C

6.CSIR-NET-DEC-2016

What is the next pattern in the given sequence?

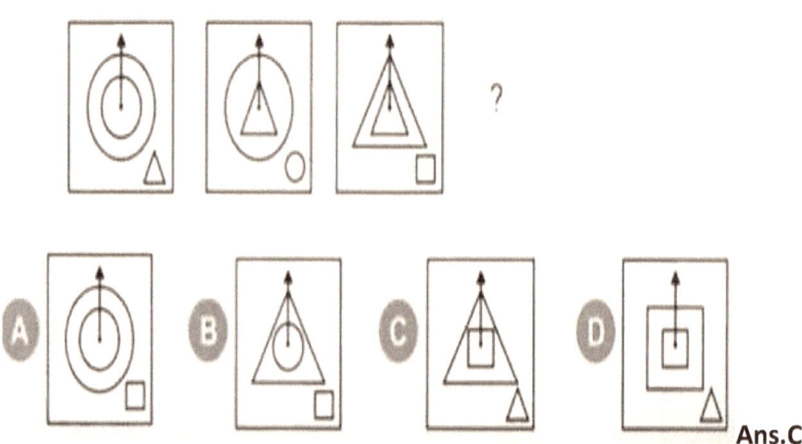

Ans.C

7.CSIR-NET-DEC-2016

Find the missing term

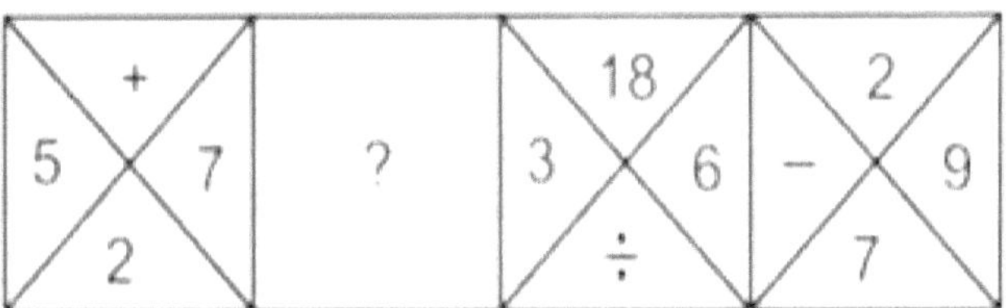

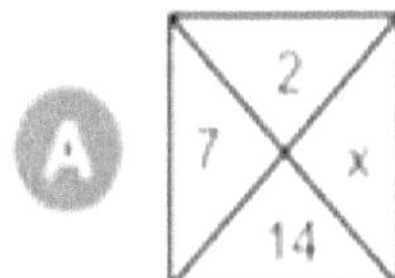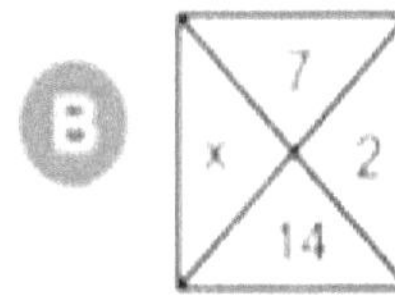

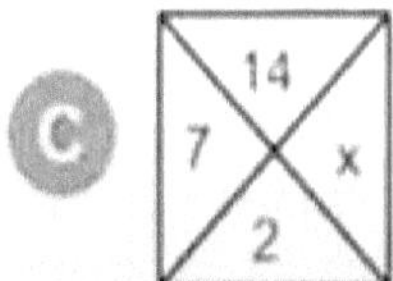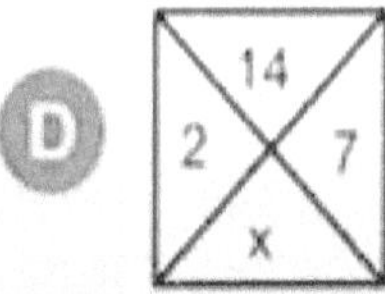

Ans.A

8. CSIR-NET-JUN-2016

What will be the next figure in the following sequence?

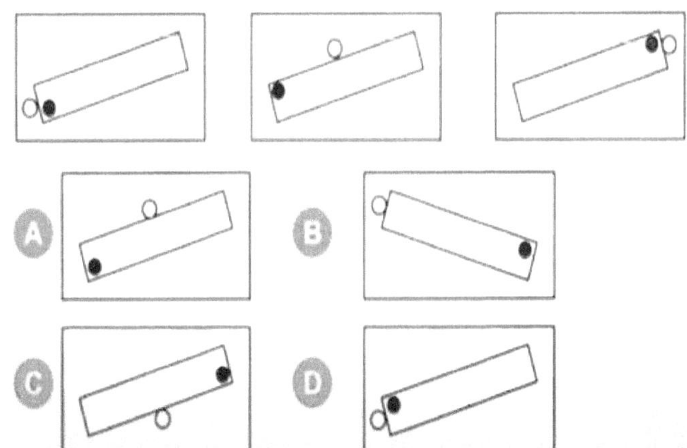

Ans.C

9. CSIR-NET-JUN-2016

Find the next figure "D"

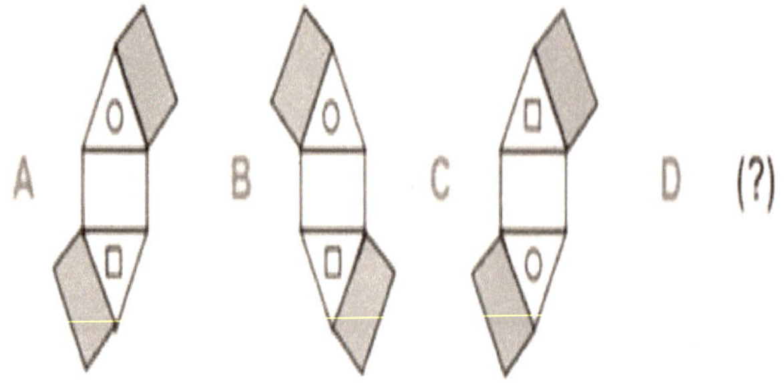

A   B   C   D   (?)

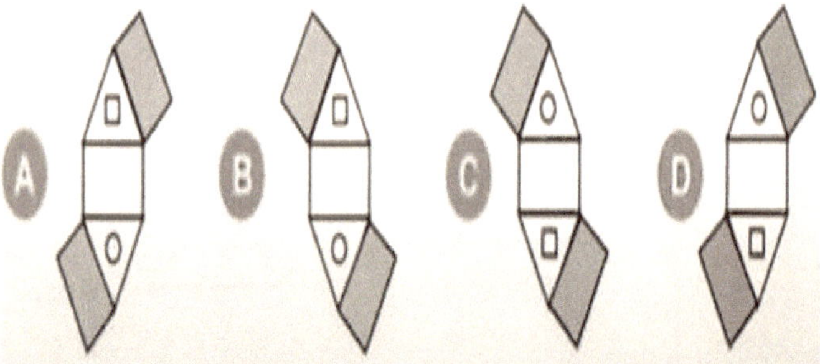

A   B   C   D

Ans.B

10. CSIR-NET-JUN-2016

The relationship among the numbers in each corner square is the same as that in the other corner squares. Find the missing number

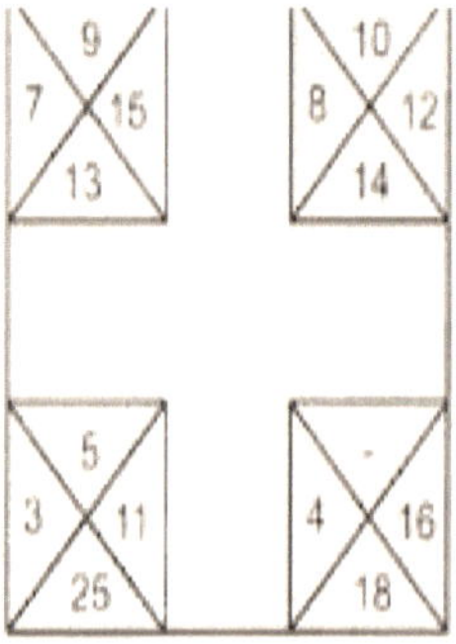

A 10   **B** 8

C 6   **D** 12

Ans.C

11. CSIR-NET-JUN-2017

Find the missing word : A, AB, ... , ABBABAAB

A AABB

B ABAB

C ABBA

D BAAB

Ans.C

12. CSIR-NET-DEC-2015

The missing number is

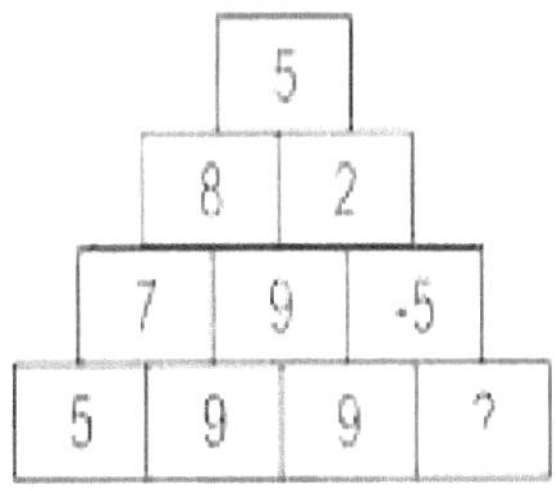

A -19

B -5

C 9

D -9

Ans.A

13. CSIR-NET-DEC-2014

Find the missing element based on the given pattern

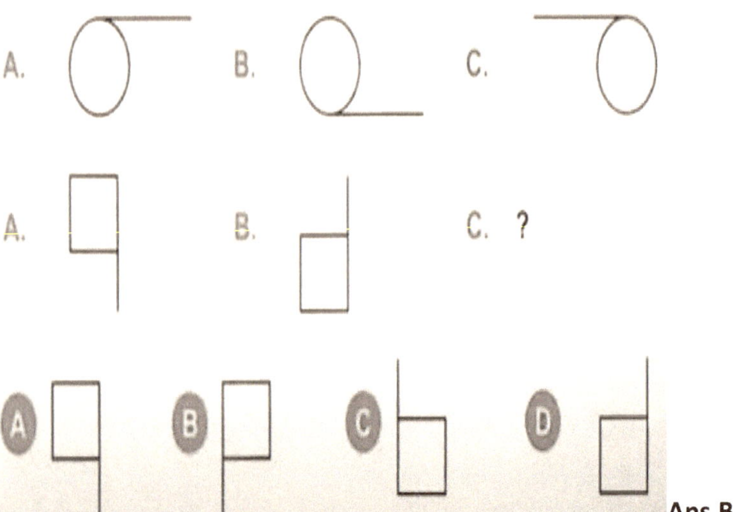

14. CSIR-NET-JUN-2016

Find the missing letter

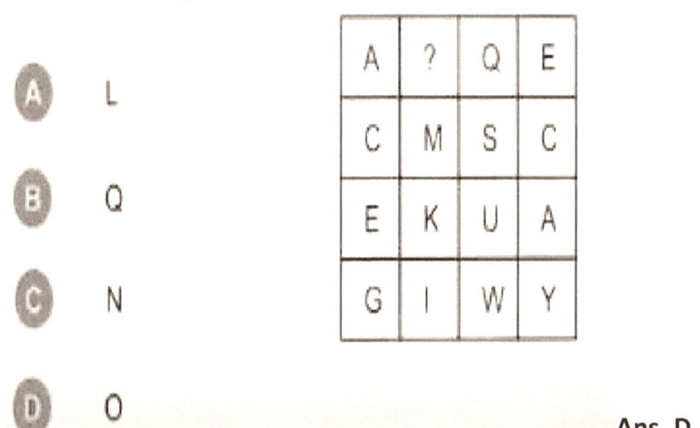

Ans. D

Hint: A-> omit B-> C -> omit D-> E -> omit F ->G->omit H -> I -> omit J -> K ->omit L -> M->omit N -> O ->omit P -> Q ------so on.

15. Find the missing letter (CSIR-NET-JUN-2014)

A B C D
F I L O
K P U Z
P W D ?

   A) P   **B) K**   C) J   D) L

Hint:- EJOTY (E->5, J->10,O->15,T->20,Y->25)

1 ->   A B C D <- 4

6 ->   F I L O <- 15

11->   K P U Z <- 26

16->   P W D ? <- 11 i.e,K

1+5->6+5->11+5->16 Likewise, 4+11->15 +11 ->26 -0+11->11(K)

16. Find the missing number in the triangle? (CSIR-NET-JUN-2014)

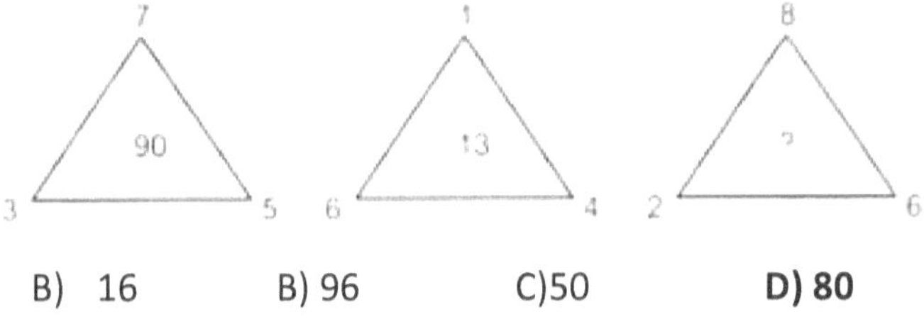

   B) 16   B) 96   C)50   **D) 80**

Hint: (3x5x7)-(3+5+7)=90 ; (6x4x1) – (6+4+1)=13 ; (2x6x8)-(2+6+8)= 96-16=80

17. What comes next in the sequence? (CSIR-NET-JUN-2013)

                                       Ans. C

A B C D E->C Option

18. Identify the next figure in the sequence? (CSIR-NET-JUN-2013)

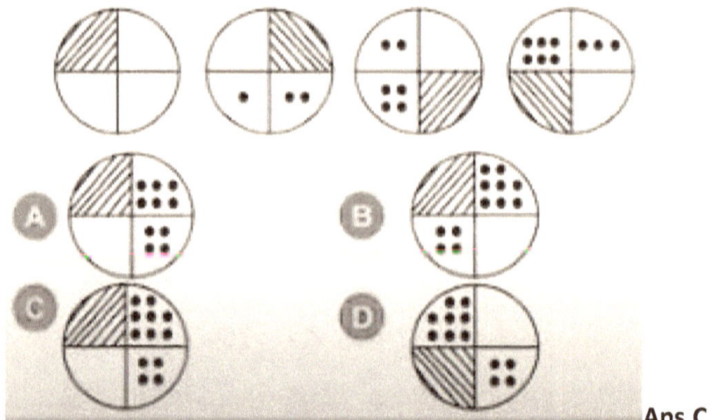

Ans.C

19.CISR-NET-DEC-2019

Find out the next figure in following sequence?

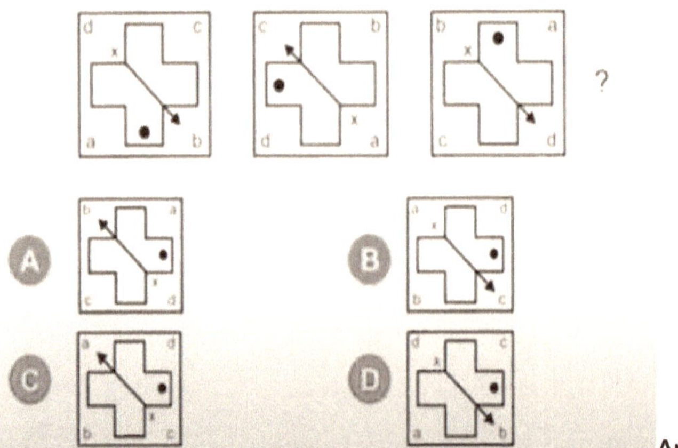

Ans.C

20.CSIR-NET-DEC-2019

Complete the figure below with the correct block.

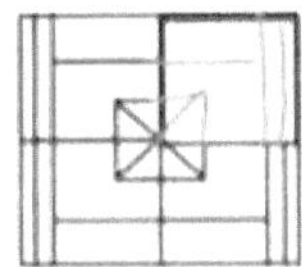

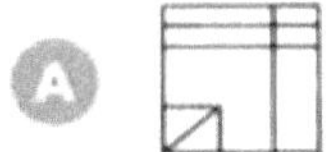

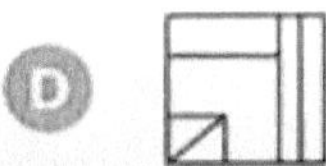

Ans.D

21. CSIR-NET-DEC-2018

Find the missing figure in the following sequence

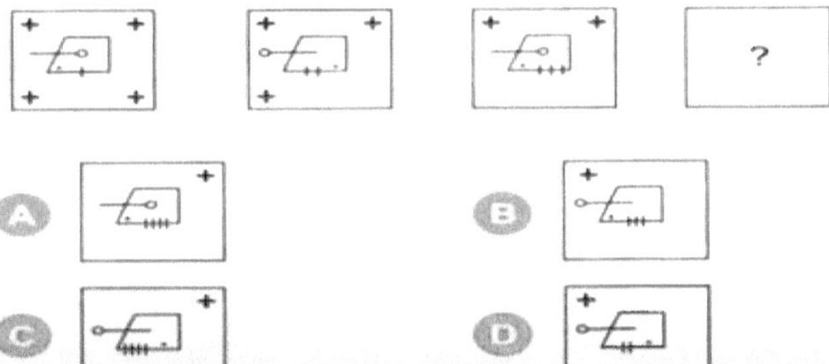

Ans.C

22. CSIR-NET-DEC-2018

What could the fourth figure in the sequence be?

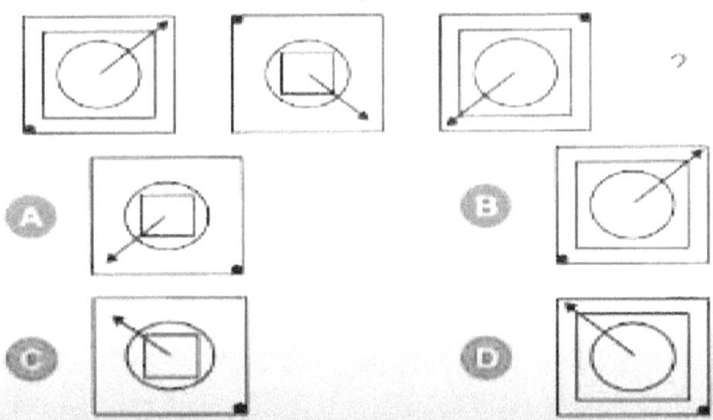

Ans.C

26. (CSIR-NET-JUN-2017)

Which of the following figures can be drawn without lifting the pen from the paper or retracing?

(A) Figure A but not figure B

(B) Figure B but not figure A

(C) Both figure A and B

(D) neither figure A nor figure B

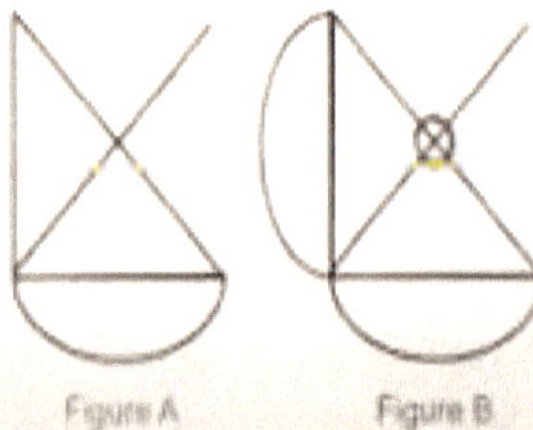

Ans.(A)

27. In a group of siblings there are seven sisters and each sister has one brother. How many siblings are there in total? (CSIR-NET-JUN-2017)

(A) 15   (B) 14   **(C) 8**   (D) 7

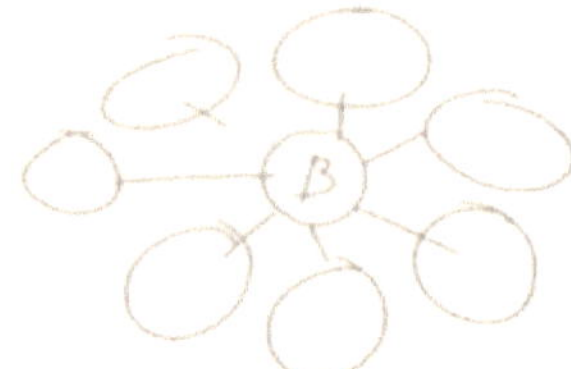

28. **185. Which among the following diagrams represent women, mothers, and human beings? (CSIR-NET-JUN-2019)**

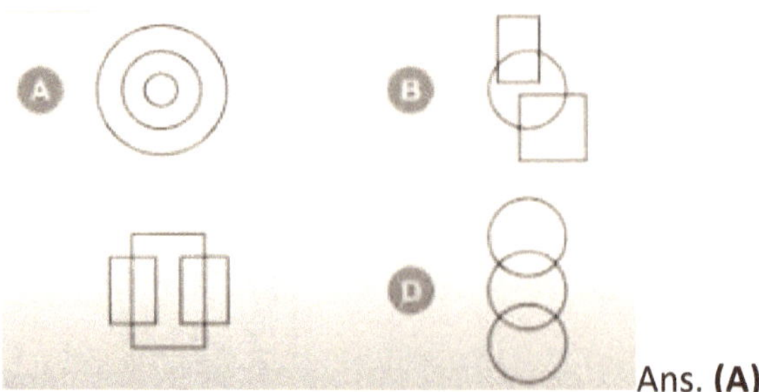

Ans. **(A)**

Mother is Woman and Woman is Human Begins.

130

29. A move of a coin is defined as crossing any number of points in a straight line on the 4 x 4 grid (horizontally, vertically or diagonally). What is the least number of moves in which a coin, starting from the indicated position, can cover all nine points within the marked square? (CSIR-NET-DEC-2019)

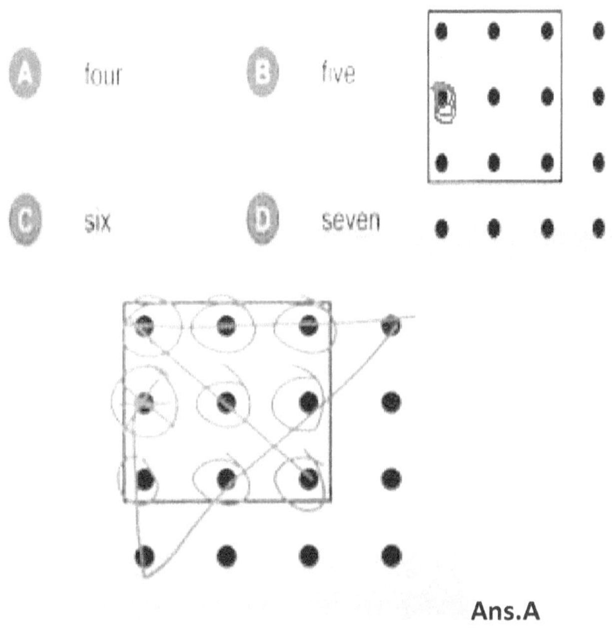

Ans.A

30. If DELHI is coded as BCJFG and MADRAS is coded as KYBPYQ then MUMBAI is coded as : ? (CSIR-NET-DEC-2019)

A) LTLAZH   B) KWNCBG   **C) KSKZYG**   D) KTKAYH

Hint: D E L H I → B C J F G (D -2 LETTER =B , E – 2LETTER =C, L – 2 LETTER =J ,H- 2 LETTER =F AND I -2 LETTER=G) ; SIMILARLY MADRAS→ KYBPYQ (M -2LETTER = K , A – 2LETTER =Y AND SO ON…..) THEREFORE, MUMBAI → M -2 LETTER = K , U – 2LETTER=S ……… So the Code word should be KSKXYG)

31. (CSIR-NET-DEC-2019)

Fact - 1 : Seeta said "Geeta and I both have cars."

Fact - 2 : Geeta said "I don't have a car."

Fact - 3 : Seeta always tells the truth, but Geeta sometimes lies.

Which of the following statement(s) must be true?

(i) Geeta has a car   (ii) Seeta has a car

(iii) Geeta is lying

(A) (i) only   (B) (i) and (ii) only

(C) (i). (ii) and (iii)   (D) Only (iii)

Ans. (C)

As Seeta always tells truth , so it is confirmed that they of both have cars, therefore both (i) and (ii) are correct again as Geeta said that she have no car , so she is telling lie, so (iii)is also correct. So, all (i) (ii) & (iii) are correct..

32. There are nine identical balls, one of which is heavier than the other eight. What is least number of weighting, using a two-pan balance needed for identifying the heavier ball?(CSIR-NET-DEC-2019)

(A) One   **(B) Two**   (C) Three   (D) Four

Divide the nine balls in three groups such that all three groups have three numbers of balls each. Now pick any two group's ball in a two-pan balance, (1) if balance is in equilibrium position then the third group's ball should be divided in three groups carrying one ball in each group. Take any two groups in balance and if it is in equilibrium position then the ball of rest group is less weighted ball. So Two times required to identify the less weighted ball. (2) if balance is not in equilibrium position then take the light group from the pan of the balance and divide the group into three groups again with one ball each and do the same process as earlier told in (1) to identify the less weighted ball. In each case two steps required to identify the less weighted ball.

33. (CSIR-NET-JUN-2018)

Suppose (i) "A*B" means "A is the father of B". (ii) "A∧B" means "A is the husband of B". (iii)" A\ B" means "A is the wife of B" and (iv) "A□ B" means "A is the sister of B". Which of the following represents "C is the father-in-law of the sister of D"?

(A) C∇E * F□D

(B) C * E∇F□D

(C) C△E * F□D

(D) C * E△F□D

Ans.(D)

Here * means father, △ means Husband, ∇ means wife and □ means Sister. C is father of husband of D's sister → Option D.

34. A librarian is arranging a thirteen – volume encyclopaedia on the shelf from left to right in the following order of volume numbers: 8, 11, 5, 4, 9, 1, 7, 6, 10, 3, 12, 2. in this pattern, where should the volume 13 be place? (CSIR-NET-JUN-2018)

(A) Leftmost   (B) Rightmost   **(C) Between 10& 3**
(D) Between 9 & 1

Eight, Eleven, Five, Four, Nine, One, Seven, Six, Ten, <u>Thirteen</u> Three, Twelve, Two. (Arrange by dictionary order)

35. If 'SELDOON' means 'NOODLES' then what does 'SPOUS' mean? (CSIR-NET-DEC-2018)

(A) SALAD   **(B) SOUPS**   (C) RASAM   (D) ONION

NOODLES is mirror image of SELDOON, So, SOUPS is the mirror image = SPOUS

TIME, DISTANCE, SPEED

1. There is a train of length 500m, in which a man is standing at the rear end. At the instant the rear end crosses a stationery observer on a platform, the man starts walking from the rear to the front and the front to the rear of the train at constant speed of 3 km/hr. The speed of the train is 80 km/hr. the distance of the man from the observer at the end of 30 minutes is? (CSIR-NET-JUN-2014)

a) 41.5 km   **b) 40.5 km**   c) 40.0 km   d) 41 km

Hint: In 30 minutes The train runs 80*1/2=40km   and the man travels =3*1/2=1.5 km but the length of the train =500m, so at 1.5km the man will be at front position (1.5km=1500m i.e, Rear to front 500m then front to rear 500m again Rear to front 500m). So the distance of the man in the train with stationery observer is 40 km+ 500m=40.5km

2. Brothers Santa and Chris walk to school from their house. The former takes 40 minutes while the latter, 30minutes. One day Santa started 5 minutes earlier than Chris. In how many minutes would Chris overtake Santa? (CSIR-NET-JUN-2016)

a) 5   **b) 15**   c) 20 d   ) 25

Hint: Let the distance between House & School is k unit. Speed of Santa is k/40 and speed of Chris is k/30, So the difference of speed =k/30 − k/40= k/120. In five minutes Santa travel distance = D=S*T=(k/40) * 5 =k/8. Now Chris overtake Santa =(k/120)*(k/8)=15

3. A person walks downhill at 10 km/hr, uphill at 6 km/hr and on the plane at 7.5 km/hr. If the person takes 3 hours to go from place A to another place B, and 1 hour on the way back, the distance between A and B is? (CSIR-NET-DEC-2015)

a) 15 km   b) 23.5 km   c) 16 km   d) Given data is insufficient to calculate the distance.

Hint:

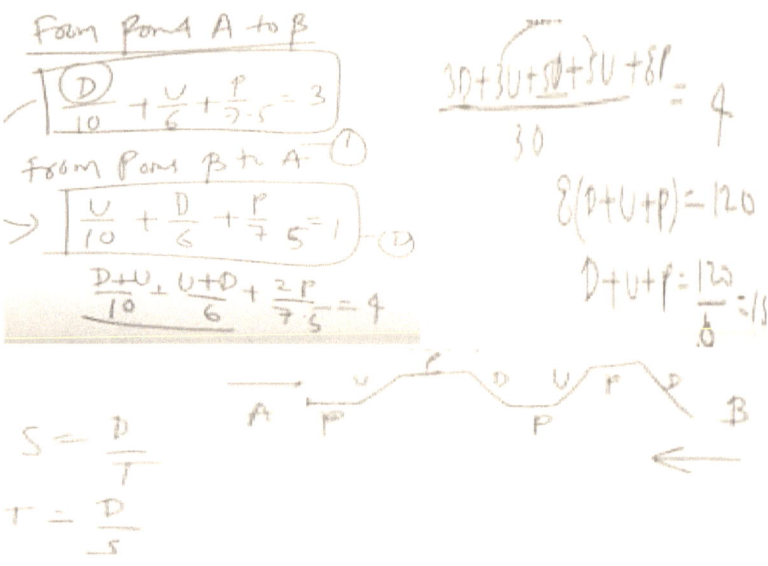

4. A float is drifting in a river, 10 m downstream of a boat that can be rowed at a speed of 10 m/minute in still water. If the boat is rowed downstream, the time taken to catch up with the float. (CSIR-NET-JUN-2015)

A) will be 1 minute   B) will be more than 1 minute   C) will be less than 1 minute D) can be determined only if the speed of the river is known.

Hint:

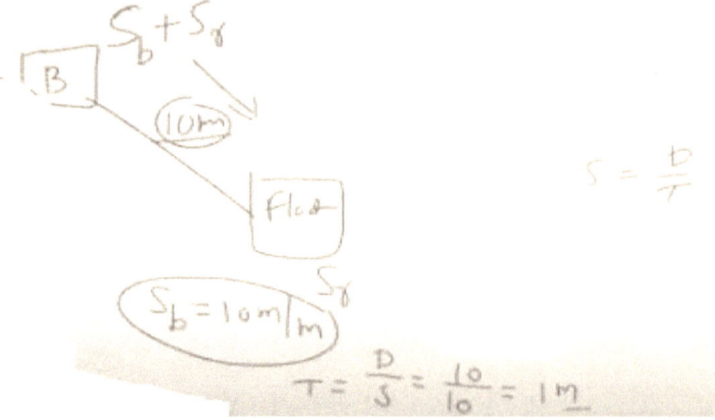

Boat have Own speed and stream speed but Float have only stream speed, it have no own speed.

5. A 3m long car goes past a 4 m long truck at rest on the road. The speed of the car is 7 m/s. The time taken to go past is? (CSIR-NET-JUN-2015)

a) 4/7 s   **b) 1 s**   c) 7/4 s   d) 10/7 s

Hint: Total distance travel = 3m + 4m =7m , speed 7m/s , so T=D/S=7/7=1 s

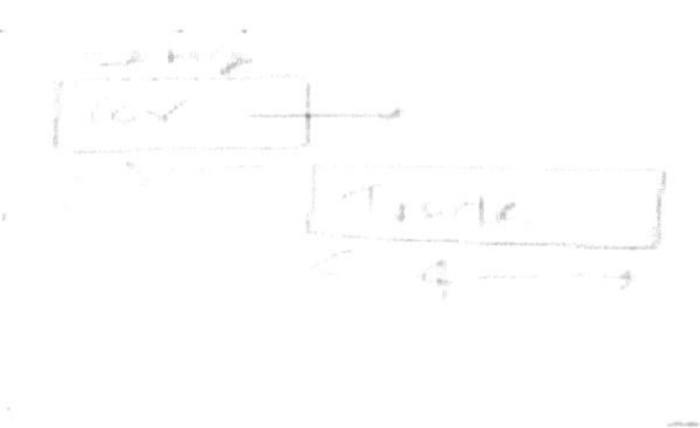

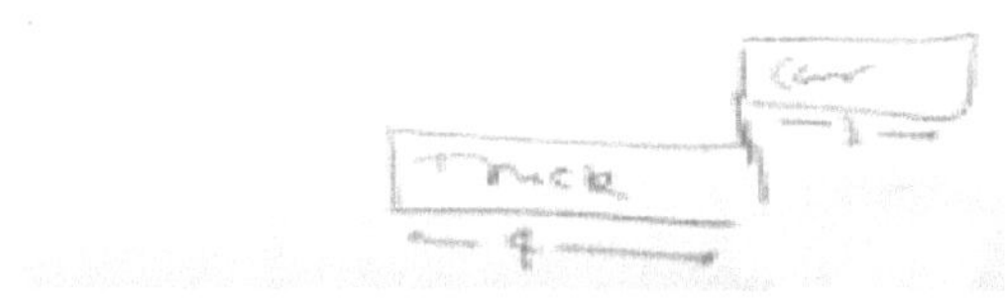

6. Two locomotives are running towards each other with speeds of 60 and 40 km/hr. An object keeps on flying to and fro from the front tip of one locomotive to the front tip off the other hand with a speed of 70 km/hr. After 30 minutes, the two locomotives collide and the object is crushed. What distance did the object cover before being crushed? (CSIR-NET-DEC-2014)

a) 50 km   b) 45 km   **c) 35 km**   d) 10 km

Hint: D=S*T , Here the speed of object =70km/hr and time=30m=1/2hr , D=70 * ½=35 km

7. To go from engine to the last coach of his train of length 200 m, a man jumped from his train to another train moving on a parallel track in the opposite direction, wanted till the last coach of his original train appeared and then jumped back. In how much time did he reach the last coach if the speed of each train was 60 km/hr? (CSIR-NET-JUN-2014)

a) 5s   **b) 6s**   c) 10s   d) 12s

Hint: We have to Find Time, T=D/S ,D=200m=.2 km , S=60 +60 = 120 km/hr Now T=0.2/120=1/600 hr=(1/600)*60*60 second=6 S

8. It takes 5 days for a steamboat to travel from A to B along a river. It takes 7 days to return from B to A . How many days will it take for a raft to drift from A to B (all speeds stay constant)? (CSIR-NET-JUN-2016)

a) 13   **b) 35**   c) 6   d) 12

Hint:

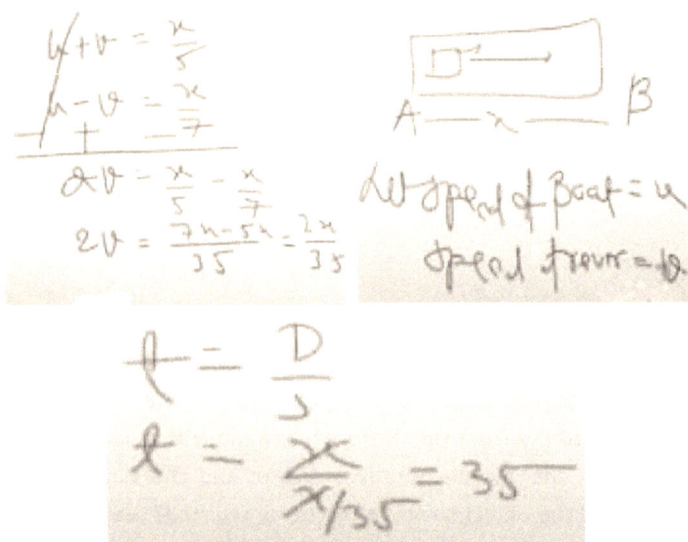

V=x/35

9. If a person travels x% faster than normal, he reaches y minutes earlier than normal. What is his normal time of travel? (CSIR-NET-DEC-2016)

a) **(100/x   + 1) y minutes** b) (x/100   +1) y minutes   c) (y/100 +1) x minutes   d) (100/7   +1) x minutes

Hint:

Let normal speed =S & time required=t, D=St , Now S= (100+x/100)S (When speed is 100 then speed increases x, therefore when speed is S then speed increases is x/100 *S)and t=t-y, St =(100+x)/100S(t-y), 100t=(100+x)(t-y) , 100t=100t-100y+xt-xy,xt=100y + xy=y(100+x) , t=(100/x +1)y

10. A and B walk up an escalator one step at a time, while the escalator itself moves up at a constant speed. A walks twice as fast as B. A reaches the top in 40 steps and B in 30 steps. How many steps of the escalator can be seen when it is not moving? (CSIR-NET-DEC-2016)

a) 30 b) 40 c) 50 **d) 60**

Hint:

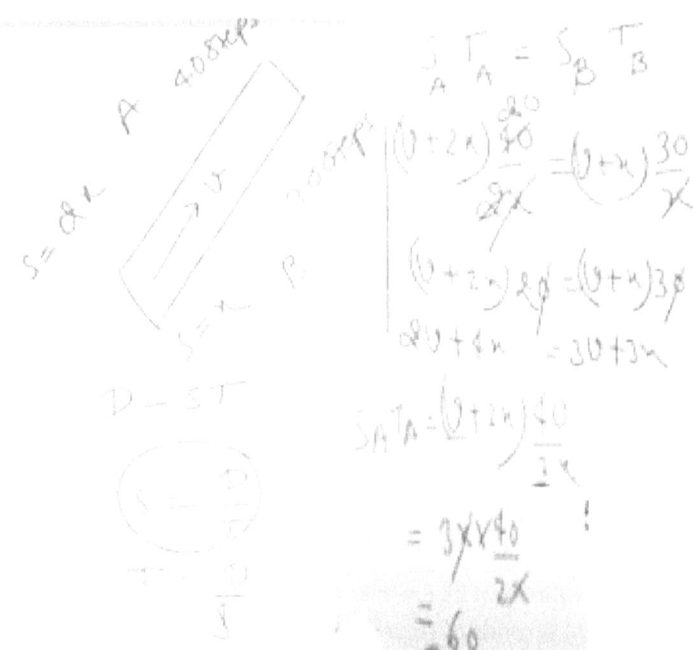

11. The distance between X and Y is 1000km. A person flies from X at 8 AM local time and reaches Y at 10 AM local time. He flies back after a halt of 4 hours at Y and reaches X at 4 PM local time on the same day. What is his average speed for the duration he is in the air? (CSIR-NET-DEC-2016)

a) 500 km/hour b) 250 km/hour c) 750 km/hour d) Cannot be calculated with the given information

Hint: A person flies from X at 8 AM and reaches Y at 10 AM, So the flies time =2 Hour , similarly after a halt of 4 hours at Y and reaches X at 4

PM , i.e. started from Y at 2 p.m.(10 a.m. + 4 hours) and reaches at 4 p.m. , so time spent is 2 hours. So total distance travel is 1000+1000=2000 km and total time spent is 2+ 2 =4 hr , The average Speed will be (2000/4) =500 km/hr

12. Abdul travels thrice the distance Catherine travels, which is also twice the distance that Binoy travels. Catherine's speed is 1/3 of Abdul's speed, which is also ½ of Binoy's speed. If they start at the same time, then who reaches first? (CSIR-NET-JUN-2016)

a) Both Abdul and Catherine   **b) Binoy**   c) Catherine   d) All three together

Hint:

Name	Distance(D)	Speed(S)	Time(T)=D/S	Ratio of Time
Binoy	x	y	x/y	x/y : 4x/y:6x/y= 1:4:6
Abdul	2x	y/2	2x/(y/2)=4x/y	So, Binoy reaches first
Catherin	6x	y/6	6x/(y/6)=36x/y	

13. A train running at 36 km/h crosses a mark on the platform in 8 seconds and takes 20 seconds to cross the platform. What is the length of the platform? (CSIR-NET-JUN-2016)

a) 120 m   b) 280 m   c) 40 m   d) 160m

Hint: As per question, the distance of the train =(36/100 *100)*8 = 2/25km = (2/25)*1000=80 m ;Similarly , the distance of the platform and train ==(36/100 *100)*20= .2km   = (.2)*1000=200 m ; So, the distance of Platform = 200-80=120m

14. A 100 m long train crosses a 200m long and 20m wide bridge in 20 seconds. What is the speed of the train in km/hr? (CSIR-NET-JUN-2017)

a) 45   b) 36   **c) 54**   d) 57.6

Hint: Distance travel= distance of Bridge + Distance of train=200 +100 =300 m = .3 km

Time taken = 20 sec= 20 * 1/60 * 1/60 =1/180, Speed= D/T=.3/(1/180)=54

15. Two persons A and B start walking in opposite directions from a point. A travels twice as fast as B. The speed at which B travels is 1 km/h. If A travels 2 km and turns back and starts walking towards B, at what distance from the starting point will A cross B?(CSIR-NET-DEC-2018)

a) 2 km   **b) 4km**   c) 6 km   d) 8 km

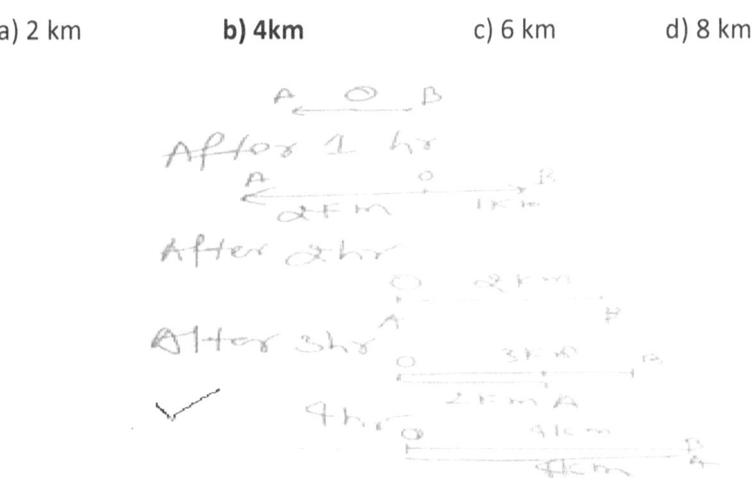

16. A person wanted to travel from Charbag to Alambag with an average speed of 60 km/h by car. The distance between Charbag and Alambag is 2 km. Due to heavy traffic; he could travel at 30 km/h for the first kilometre of his journey. What should his speed be for the remaining journey to achieve his average speed target by 60 km/h? (CSIR-NET-DEC-2018) (Hint- 2 $S_1 S_2/S_1 + S_2$)

a) Cannot achieve his target with any finite speed.   b) 60 km/h   c) 90 km/h   d) 120 km/h

Hint:

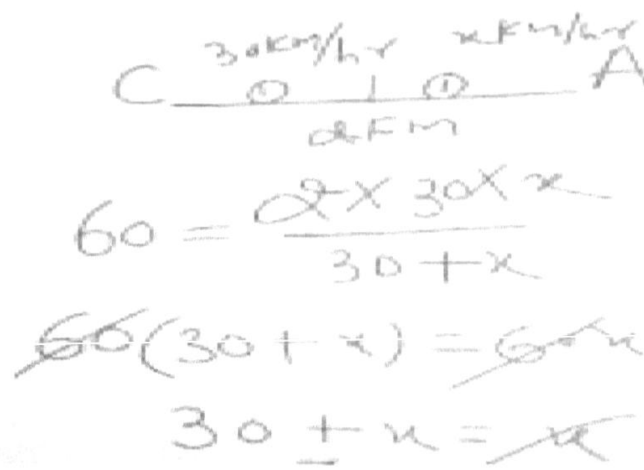

17. Two runners A and B running from diametrically opposite points on a circular track in the same direction. If A runs at a constant speed of 8 km /h and B at a constant of 6 km/h and A catches up with B in 30 minutes, what is the length of the track? (CSIR-NET-DEC-2018)

a) 1 km   b) 4km   c) 3 km   **d) 2 km**

Hint:

In 30 minutes A Run (8/60)*30 = 4 km and B runs (6/60)*30 = 3 km. As A and B running from diametrically opposite points on a circular track then it is clear that the half Track travels by A is (4 − 3)=1 km and therefor length of full track will be 1*2=2 km.

18. The distance from Nehrunagar to Gandhinagar is 27 km. A and B start walking from Nehrunagar towards Gandhinagar at speeds of 5 km/hr and 7 km/hr, respectively. B reaches Gandhinagar, returns immediately and meats A at Indiranagar. What is the distance between Nehrunagar and Indiranagar? What is the distance between Nehrunagar and Indiranagar? (Assume all three cities to be in one straight line). (CSIR-NET-DEC-2017)

a) 12.5 km   **b) 22.5km**   c) 4.5 km   d) 13.5 km

Hint:

Suppose the distance between Gandhinagar to Indiranagar = x km and given that the distance between Nehrunagar to Gandhinagar is 27 km. So, the distance between Nehrunagar to Indiranagar is (27-x) km. Now A reaches Indiranagar =1/5 *(27-x) and   B reaches =1/7 *(27+x) and therefore, 1/5 *(27-x) =1/7 *(27+x) or, 189-7x=135+5x or, 12x =54, or x=54/12=4.5, so, the distance between Nehrunagar to Indiranagar is =27-4.5=22.5 km

19. Walking from my home at a speed of 5 km/h, I am 8 minutes late in reaching my Office. If I walk at a speed of 8 km/h, I reach 5 minutes late. How far is my office from the house? (CSIR-NET-JUN-2017)

a) 2 km   b) 1/3 km   **c) 2/3 km**   d) 1/2 km

Hint:

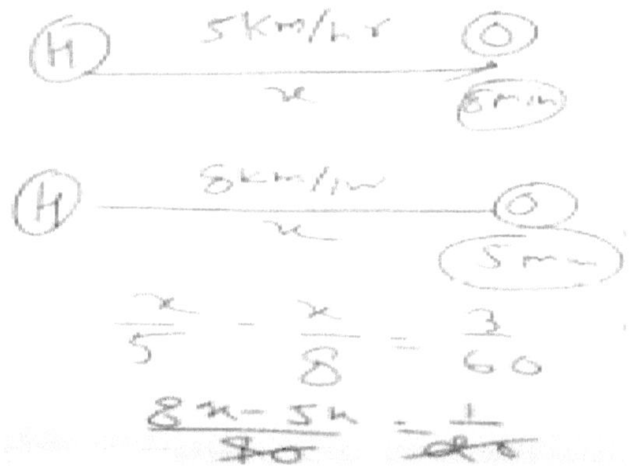

Therefore, 3x=2 , or x= 2/3

20. Two runners starting together run on a path taking 6 and 8 minutes, respectively, to complete one round. How many minutes later do they meet again for the first time on the start line, assuming constant speeds. (CSIR-NET-JUN-2019)

a) 8   **b) 24**   c) 32   d) 60

Hint:

1ST RUNNER	2nd RUNNER
0-6	0-8
6-12	8-16
12-18	16-24
18-24	

21. In a 100 m race A beats B by 10 m. B beats C by 5 m. By how many meters does A beats C? (CSIR-NET-JUN-2018)

(A) 15.0 m　　　　(B) 5.5 m　　　　(C) 10.5 m　　　　**(D) 14.5 m**

Hint: When A travels → 100m ,then B travels 90 m .Again when B travels 100m then C travels 95: therefore when b travels 90 m then C travels (95/100)*90=85.5m , So, A beats C by 100-85.5=14.5 m

Miscellaneous

1. A new tyre can be used for at most 90km. What is the maximum distance (in km) that can be covered by a three wheeled vehicle carrying one spare wheel, all four tyres being new? (CSIR-NET-DEC-2017)

A) 180   **(B) 90**   (C) 120   (D) 270

Hint:

Tyre 1	Tyre 2	Tyre 3	Tyre 4	
30	30	30	---	90
---	30	30	30	90
30	---	30	30	90
30	30	---	30	90
90	90	90	90	

2. In a group of students, 30% play only cricket, 20% play only football and 10% play only basketball. 20% of the students play both football and cricket, 15% play both basketball and cricket, 10% play both football and basketball.15 students play no games, while 5% of the students play all three games. What is the total number of students? (CSIR-NET-JUN-2017)

A) 300   (B) 250   (C) 350   (D) 400

Hint:

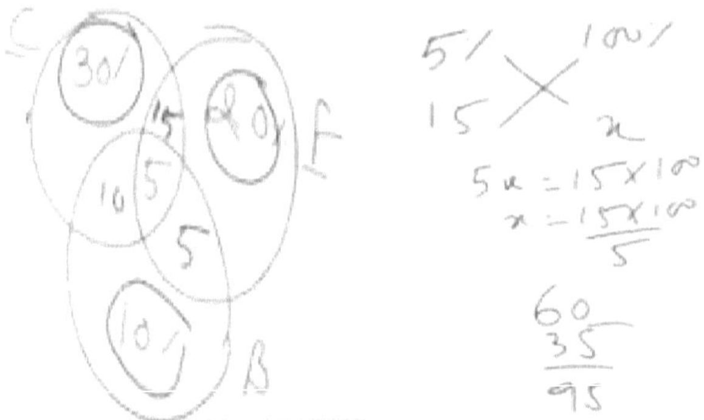

3. A cylindrical cake is to be cut into 16 equal pieces. What is the minimum number of cuts required to do so? (CSIR-NET-JUN-2017)

(A) 9   (B) 3   (C) 8   **(D) 5**

Hint:

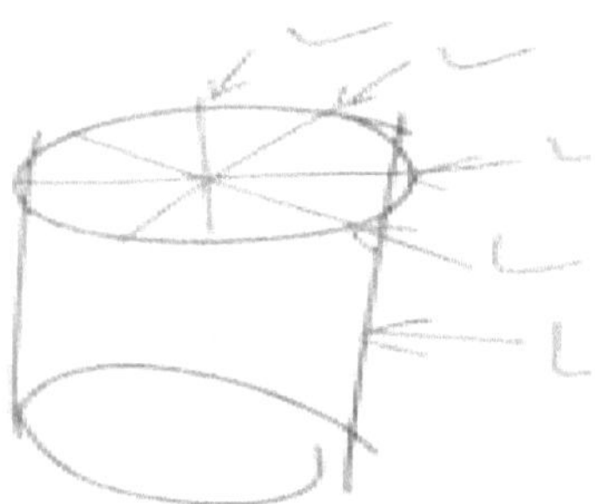

4. If equal weights of 22 carat gold (alloy of 22 parts gold and 2 parts copper by weight) and 24 carat gold (pure gold) are mixed to form an alloy, what will be the weight proportion of copper in the alloy? (CSIR-NET-JUN-2017)

(A) 1/2   (B) 1/8   (C) 1/12   **(D) 1/24**

Hint: After mixing total alloy will be 24 + 24= 48 carat and in this 48 carat 2 carat will be copper. So the proportion of copper in the alloy will be 2/48= 1/24

5. A 4m x 4m floor needs to be covered by tiles of size 2m x 1m. Two diagonally opposite corners of size 1m x 1m should be left uncovered. How many tiles are required to complete the job without breaking the tiles or overlapping them? (CSIR-NET-JUN-2017)

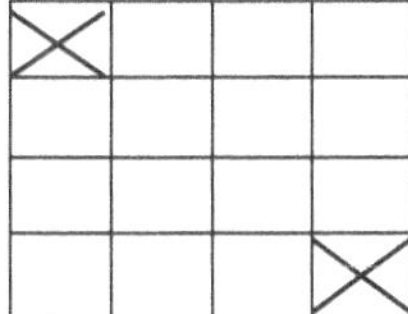

(A) 6   (B) 7   (C) 8   **(D) Impossible to cover**

6. An ant starts at the origin and moves along the y-axis and covers a distance l . This is the first stage in its journey. Every subsequent stage requires the ant to turn right and move a distance which is half of its previous stage. What would be its coordinates at the end of its 5th stage? (CSIR-NET-JUN-2017)

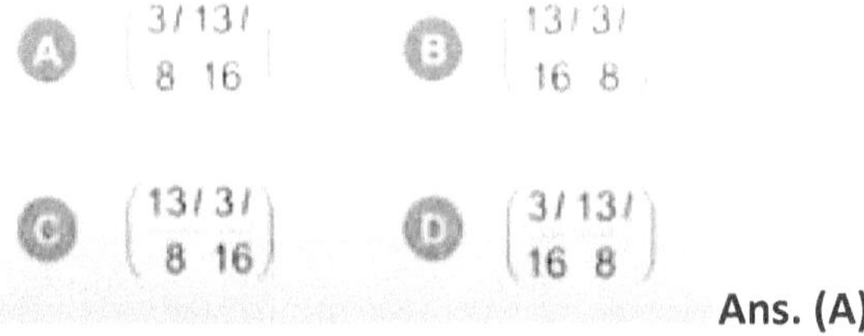

Ans. (A)

Hint:

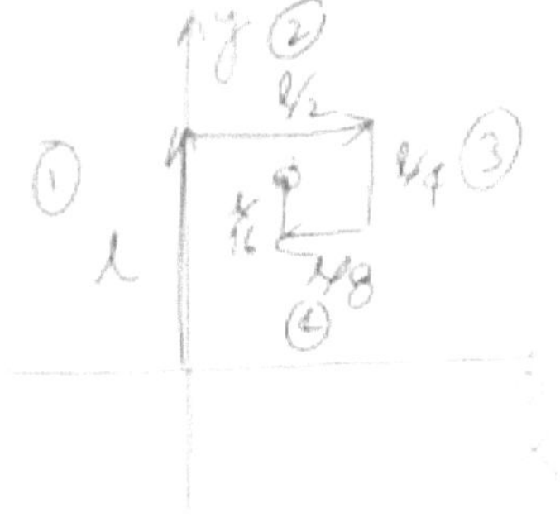

Here X coordinates will be (after 5th stage) = l/2 - l/8 = (4l -l) /8 =3l/8

Again Y coordinates will be (after 5th stage) = l - l/4 + l/16= (16l -4l + l) /16 =13l/16

7. What is the volume of soil in an open pit of size 2m x2m x 10 cm? (CSIR-NET-DEC-2017)

(A) $4m^3$ (B) $0.4m^3$ **(C) 0 m^3**   (D)$4.0m^3$

Hint: **Open pit is** denoting a method of mining in which coal or ore is extracted at or from a level near the earth's surface, rather than from shafts; opencast. So open pit should have no volume of soil.

8. Nine-eleventh of the members of a parliamentary committee is men. Of the men, two-thirds are from the Rajya Sabha. Further, 7/11 of the total committee members are from Rajya Sabha. What fraction of the total number are women from the Lok Sabha? (CSIR-NET-JUN-2018)

(A) 1/11   (B) 6/11   (C) 2/11   (D) 3/11

	RS	LS	TOT
MEN	2/3 * 9/11= 6/11	(9/11 - 6/11)= 3/11	9/11
WOMEN	1/11	1/11	2/11
TOT	7/11	4/11	11/11

9. When a farmer was asked as to how many animals he had, he replied that all but two were cows, all but two were horses and all but two were pigs. How many animals did he have? (CSIR-NET-JUN-2018)

(A) 3   (B) 6   (C) 8   (D) 12

Hint: Let the farmer have total x animals, then cow=x − 2, Horse = x -2 Pig = x-2, Therefore x-2+x-2+x-2 =x,

3x-6=x , 2x=6, x=3

10. The number of three English words, having at least one consonant, but not having two consecutive constants, is (CSIR-NET-DEC-2017)

a) 2205 **b) 3780** c) 2730 d) 3360

There is 21 consonant   5 vowels in English letter.

C	V	V	21 X 5 X 5	= 525
V	C	V	5 X 21 X 5	=525
V	V	C	5 X 5 X 21	=525
C	V	C	21 X 5 X 21	=2205
				3780

11. In how many distinguishable ways can the letters of the word CHANCE be arranged? (CSIR-NET-DEC-2016)

a) 120 b) 720 **c) 360** d) 240

CHANCE HAS 6 DIGITS AND C TWO TIMES REAPETING DIGIT. THER FORE 6! /2! =720/2 = 360

12. Consider a series of a letters placed in the following way: U_G_C_C_S_I_R . Each letter moves one step to its right and the extreme right letter takes the first position, completing one operation. After which of the following numbers of operations does the Cs not sit side by side? (CSIR-NET-JUN-2015)

a) 3 b) 10 c) 19 **d) 25**

U_G_C_C_S_I_R -→ R_U_G_C_C_S_I →I_R_U_G_C_C_S →
S_I_R_U_G_C_C→C_S_I_R

_U_G_C   4 → 11 → 18 → 25

13. A code consists of at most two identical letters followed by at most four identical digits. The code must have at least one letter and one digit. How many distinct codes can be generated using letters A to Z and digits 1 to 9? (CSIR-NET-DEC-2014)

a) 936 b) 1148 **c) 1872** d) 2574

As the code must have at least one letter and one digit and there should be at most 2 identical letters followed by at most four identical digits then the possibility of codes must be 8.

LD , LDD,LDDD,LDDDD ; LLD , LLDD, LLDDD ; LLDDDD --→ 8 possibility

AA, BB, ..., ZZ AND   1111,2222,...........,9999(Here We have 26 alphabets and number 9).

So, distinct codes can be generated using letters A to Z and digits 1 to 9 = 26 x 9 x 8 =26 x 72 =1872

14. A mouse has to go from a point A to B without retracing any part of the path, and never moving backwards. What is the total number of distinct paths that the mouse may take to go from A to B? (CSIR-NET-DEC-2014)

a) 11   **b) 48**   c) 72   d) 24

Path 2 x 4 x3 x 2 =48

15. A farmer gives 7 Full, 7 half-full and 7 empty bottles of honey to his three sons and asks them to share these among themselves such that each of them gets the same amount of honey and the same number of bottles. In how many ways can this be done? (Bottles cannot be distinguished otherwise; they are sealed and cannot be broken)(CSIR-NET)

a) 0   b) 1   **c) 2**   d) 3

If one bottle have 1 litre honey then total honey will be 7+3.5 =10.5 , so Every son have to be distributed 10.5/3 = 3.5 l honey and 7 bottle each. Now we see the possibility

2F   3HF   2E
2F   3HF   2E
3F   1HF   3F

3F 1HF 3E
3F 1HF 3E

1F 5HF 3E

16. During a summer vacation, of 20 friends from a hostel, each wrote a letter to each of all others. The total number of letters written was (CSIR-NET-JUN-2013)

a) 20   b) 400   c) 200   **d) 380**

20 X 19 =380

17. The number of squares in the figures is **(CSIR-NET-DEC-2015)**

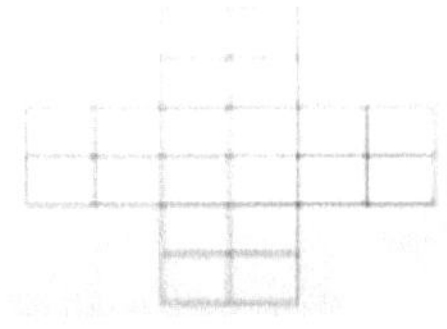

a) 30   **b) 29** c) 25   d) 20

Geometry

1. The Number of triangle in the figure is? (CSIR-NET-DEC-2019)

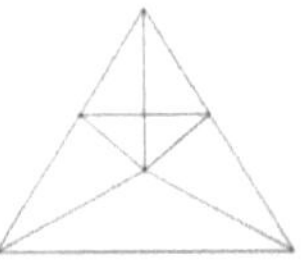

a) 9　　　　b) 10　　　　c) 11　　　　**d) 12**

2. A, B, C and D are four consecutive points on a circle such that chords AB=BC=CD=10.0 cm and DA=20.0cm. The radius of the circle (in cm) is? (CSIR-NET-DEC-2019)

a) 10.0　b) 10/2　c) 13/3　d) 20.0

3. Pick the correct statement. (CSIR-NET-DEC-2019)

a) The sum of any two sides of a plane triangle is always less than third side.

b) The sum of squares of two sides of a plane triangle is always equal to the square of third side.

c) Two internal angles of a scalene plane triangle can be equal.

d) The sum of the internal angle (in radians) of a plane triangle is the same as the ratio of the circumference of a circle to its diameter.(Π = 2πr/2r)

4. In the trapezium ABCD, what is the length of CP? (CSIR-NET-DEC-2019)

A　　4　　　　　B　　$4\sqrt{3}$

C　　3　　　　　D　　$3\sqrt{3}$

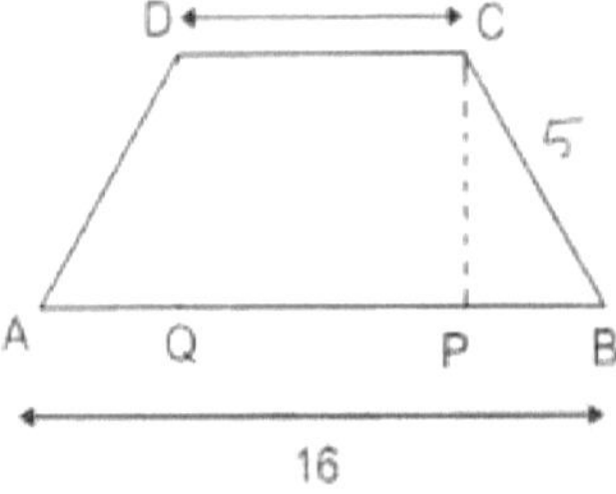

Ans.A

DC = QP = 10 CM , AB – QP = 16- 10 = 6 , AQ=PB=3 , $CP^2 = BC^2 – PB^2 = 25 – 9$ =16 =4^2 , CP = 4

5. In the following figure, E is midpoint of Df,FGHI is square and EIF is an equilateral triangle. What is area of square FGHI? (CSIR-NET-DEC-2019)

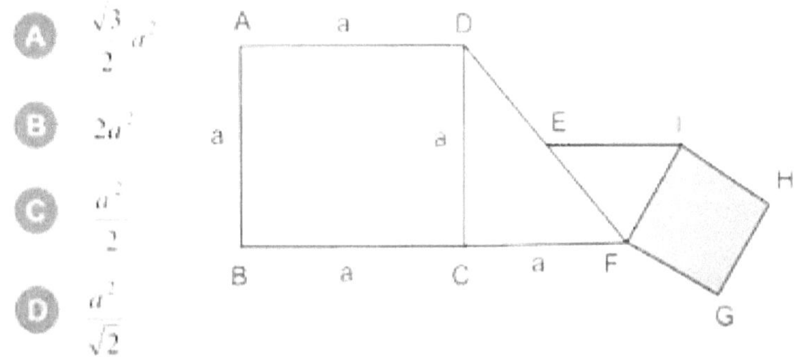

Ans. C

$(DF)2 = a^2 + a^2 = 2a^2$, DF = $root\ of$ 2 x a , EF= DF/2 = root of 2 x a /2 = a / root of 2=IF=HI+HG=GF

The area of square IFGH = a / root of 2 x a / root of 2= a^2 / 2

6. Which of the following is true for the internal angles A,B and C of a plane scalene triangle? (CSIR-NET-DEC-2019)

a) tanA + tanB + tanC =0 b) tanA + tanB + tanC=1 c) tan(A+B) = tan C **d) tanA + tanB + tanC=tanA.tanB.tanC**

A + B + C =π , A + B = π –C, tan(A + B) = tan (π –C) = - tanC   , tanA + tanB / 1 – tanAtanB = -tanc

7. Out of 6 unbiased coins, 5 are tossed independently and they all results in heads. If the 6th is now independently tossed, the probability of getting heads is? (CSIR-NET-DEC-2018)

a) 1   b) 0   **c) ½**   d) 1/6

8. Two integers are picked at random from the first 15 positive integers without replacement. What is the probability that the sum of the two numbers is 20? (CSIR-NET-JUN-2013)

a) ¾   **b) 1/21**   c) 1/105   d) 1/20

$(5,15)$;$(6,14)$; $(7,13)$;$(8,12)$;$(9,11)$ = $5 / {}^{15}C_2 = 1/21$

9. ABCD is a rectangle and O is the midpoint of AD. P and Q are points on AB and Cd respectively such that AP=1/4 AB and DQ=1/4DC. The ratio of area of rectangle ABCD and triangle OPQ is ? (CSIR-NET-JUN-2019)

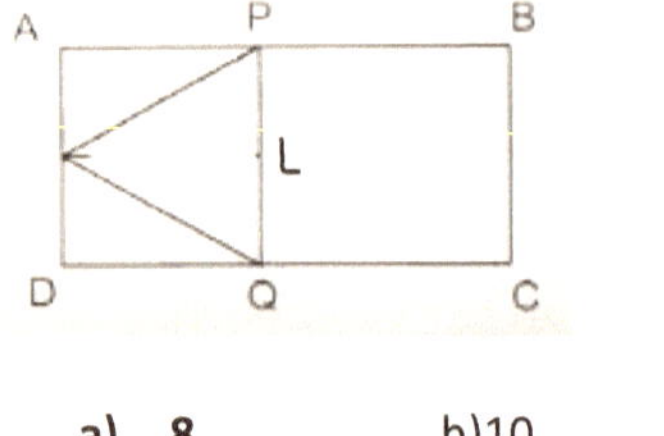

a)   **8**   b)10   c)11   d)12

Let AB = 4 then AP= (1/4)AB =1 ; Again let DC= 4 then DQ=(1/4) DC=1 ; Now assume PQ=x and as AP=DQ=1 then OL = 1; as PQ=x=BC=AD ;Therefore , Area of Rectangle ABCD / Area of Triangle OPQ = 4 x X/(1/2)*X*1 =8

10. In a given circle, O is the centre, $/\_PAO = 40^0$,$/\_PBQ = 30^0$ and the outer angle $/\_AOB = 220^0$ then $/\_AQB$ is ? (CSIR-NET-JUN-2019)

a) 70^0 b)80^0 c)60^0 d)110^0

Outer $/\_AOB = 220^0$, Then Inner $/\_AOB=360^0 -220^0 = 140^0$, Therefore $/\_AQB = /\_APB = 140^0/2 = 70^0$

We know that the inner angle on centre of a circle $/\_AOB= 2 \times /\_AQB$

11. An open rectangular box is made by excluding the four identical corners of a piece of paper as shown in the diagram and folding it along the dotted lines. The capacity of the box (in cm^3) is ? (CSIR-NET-JUN-2019)

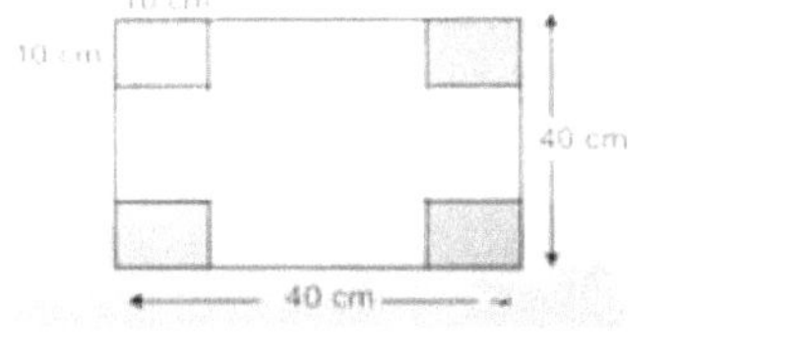

a)8000   b)1000   **c)4000**   d)6000

V = l x b x h = 20 x 20 x 10 =4000 , After folding l will be 40-10-10=20 and b will be 40-10-10=20 and Height will be 10.

12. Rectangular photo frame of size 30cm x 40cm has a photograph mounted at the center leaving a 5cm border all around. The area of the border is ? (CSIR-NET-DEC-2018)

a) 600 cm^2   b)350 cm^2 c)400 cm^2 d)700 cm^2

The area of rectangular photo frame will be 30 x 40 = 1200 cm^2

The area of Photo frame leaving the border = (30-5-5)(40-5-5)=20 x 30 =600cm^2

Therefore , area of border will be 1200cm^2 – 600cm^2= 600cm^2

13. A circular running track has six lanes, each 1m wide. How far ahead (in Meters) should the runner in the outermost lane start from , so as to cover the same distance in one lap as the runner in the innermost lane? (CSIR-NET-DEC-2018)

(A) 6 π   **(B)** 10 π

(C) 12 π   **(D)** 36 π

Ans.B

The Inner circle =2πr (r is the radius of the inner circle)

The outer circle =2π(r + 5) ; Therefore , 2π(r + 5) - 2πr =10π

14. In the context of tilling a plane surface, which of the following polygons is the odd one out? (CSIR-NET-DEC-2018)
a) Equilateral Triangle   b) Square   **c) Regular Pentagon**   d) Regular Hexagon

The angle of a polygon = (n – 2)180^0

15.A, B, C, D are points on a circle with AB=5 cm. BC =12 cm, AC = 13 cm and AD = 7 cm. Then, the closest approximation of CD is ? (CSIR-NET-JUN-2016)

a) 9 cm   b) 10 cm   **c) 11 cm**   d) 14 cm

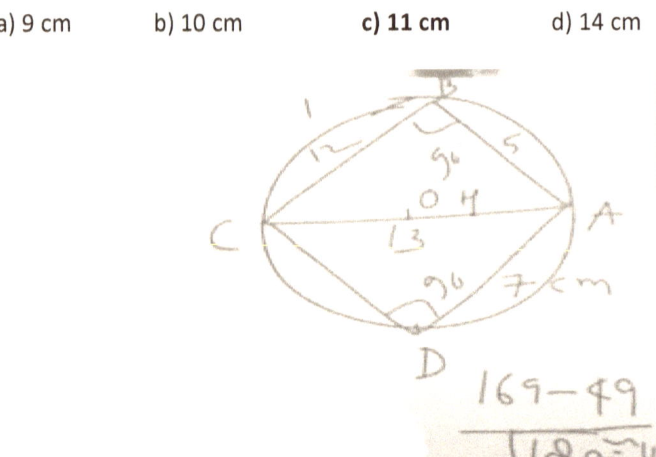

16. Consider a square of side a. Fit the largest possible circle inside it and the largest possible square inside the circle. What is the side length of the innermost square? (CSIR-NET-JUN-2016)

(a) $\dfrac{a}{\pi/2}$ (b) $\dfrac{a}{2}$ (c) $\dfrac{a}{2\sqrt{2}}$ (d) $\dfrac{a}{\sqrt{2}}$ Ans. (d)

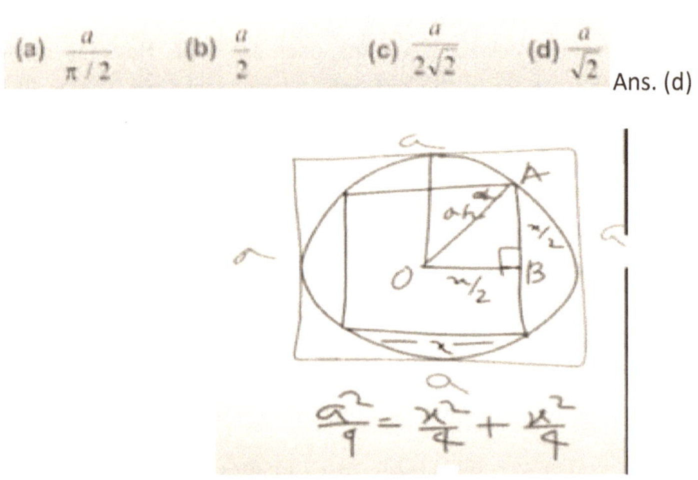

. $a^2/4 = 2x^2/4$ or $a^2 = 2x^2$ or $x^2 =a^2/2$ or x= a/ $\sqrt{2}$

17. The area of the triangle formed by joining the points (2017,2017),(2027,2027) and (2037,2017) is ? (CSIR-NET-JUN-2018)

(A) 2017　　　　　　**(B)** 100

C 100, 10　　　　　**D** 100, 20

Ans.(B)

18. In the diagram, what is the ratio of the total shaded area (of the circle and semi-circle) to the total area of the square and the rectangle? (CSIR-NET-JUN-2018)

A 5/6 π　　　　　　**B** 6/5 π

C 5/12 π　　　　　　**D** π / 4

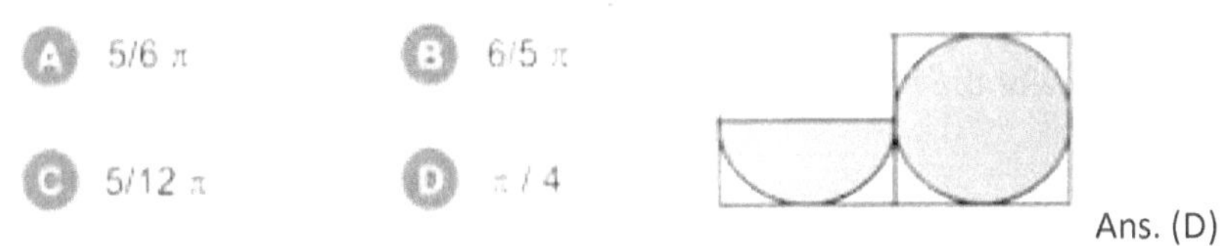

Ans. (D)

19. The smallest square floor which can be completely paved tiles of size 8x6 , without breaking any tile needs n tiles. Finds n. (CSIR-NET-JUN-2018)

a) 56　　　　**b) 12**　　　　c) 24　　　　d) 48

20. A 2m long ladder is to reach a wall of height 1.75m. The largest horizontal distance of the ladder from the wall could be --? (CSIR-NET-DEC-2017)

a) slightly less than 1m　　　b) slightly more than 1m　　c) 1m　　d) 1.2m

21. Three quarters of a circle is shown in the figure. OA and OB are two radii perpendicular to each other . C is the point on the circle. What is the angle ACB? (CSIR-NET-DEC-2017)

A cannot be determined　　　**B** 30°

C 60°　　　　　　　　　　**D** 45°

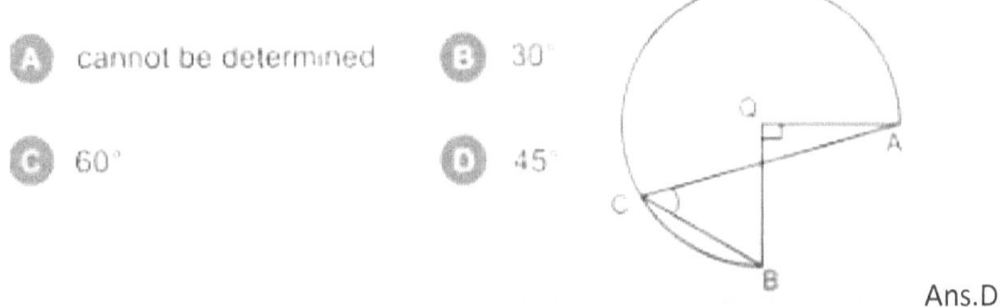

Ans.D

22. In triangle ABC, AB=AC and angle BAC = 90^0; EF||AB and DF || AC. The total area of the shaded region is? (CSIR-NET-JUN-2017)

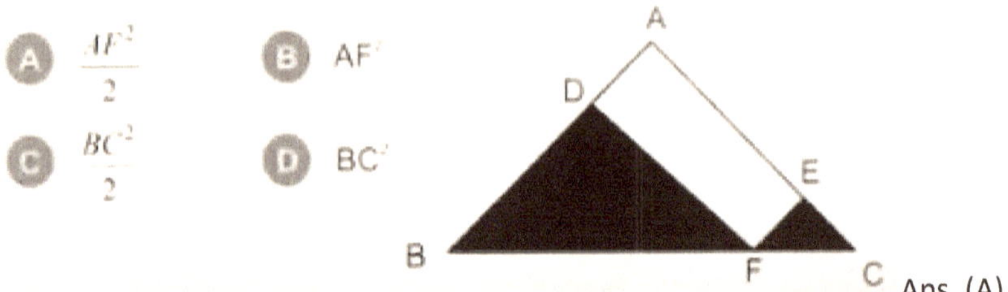

(A) $\dfrac{AF^2}{2}$ (B) AF^2

(C) $\dfrac{BC^2}{2}$ (D) BC^2

Ans. (A)

23. Areas of three parts of a rectangle are given in unit of cm^2. What is the total area of the rectangle? (CSIR-NET-DEC-2018)

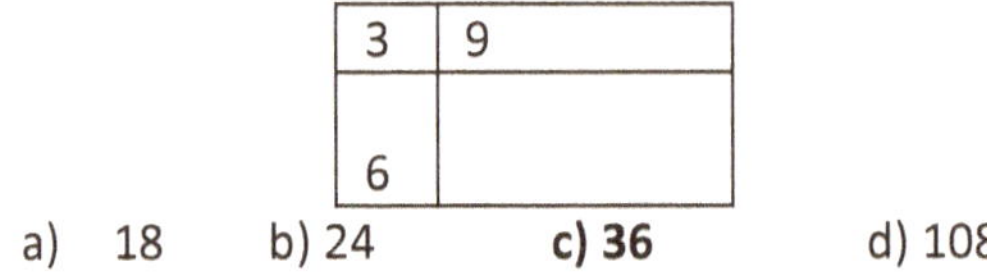

a) 18   b) 24   **c) 36**   d) 108

24. What is the total number of parallelogram in the given figure?

(a) 27   (b) 24

(c) 22   (d) 14

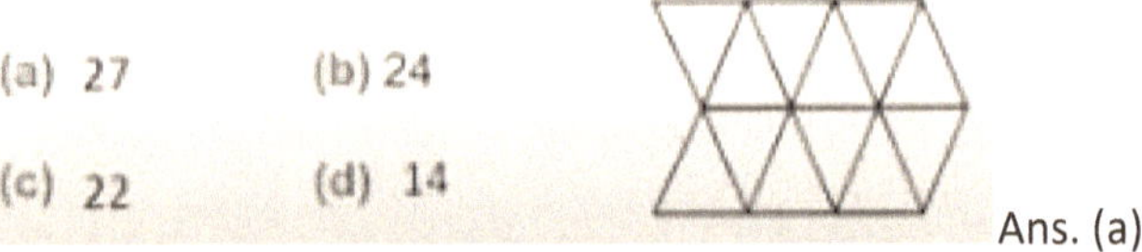

Ans. (a)

25. (CSIR-NET-DEC-2017)

DRQP is a small square of side a in the corner of a big square ABCD of side A. What is the ratio of the area of the quadrilateral PBRQ to that of the square ABCD. Given that A/a = 3 ?

(A) 2 / 9   (B) 1 / 6

(C) 1 / 3   (D) 2 / 7

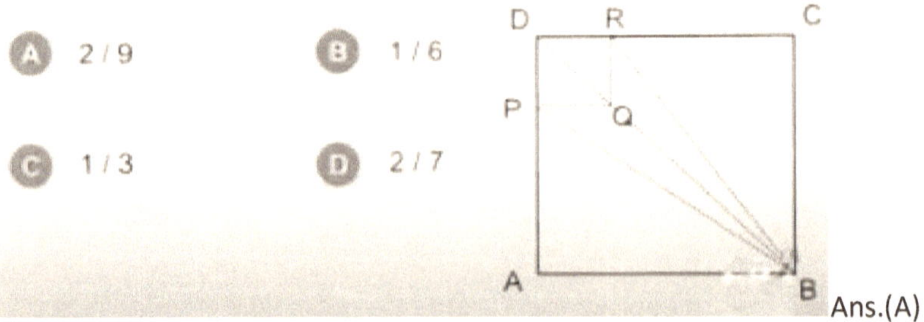

Ans.(A)

26. (CSIR-NET-JUN-2017)

158

The diagram shows a cubic block of marbles ($1 \times 1 \times 1 m^3$) having a planar fracture. What is the maximum number of slabs sized $20 \times 20 \times 5$ cm^3 that can be cut from this block avoiding the fracture?

(A) 200

(B) 300

(C) 400

(D) 500

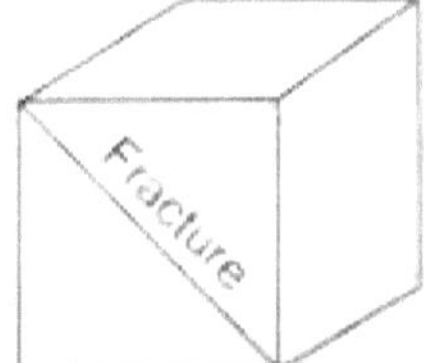

Ans.(C)

27. (CSIR-NET-DEC-2016)

OA, OB and OC are radii of the quarter circle shown in the figure AB is also equal to the radius. What is angle OCB?

(A) 60

(B) 75

(C) 55

(D) 65

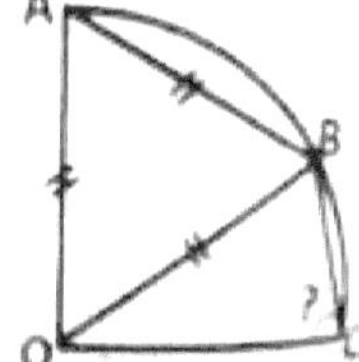

Ans.(B)

DATA INTERPRETATION

143. CSIR-NET-DEC-2019

The result of a survey to find the most preferred leader among A, B, C is shown in the table. First, second and third preferences are given weights 3, 2, 1 respectively. Statistically, which of the following can be said to represent the preferences of the voters?

(A) A and C are within 10% of each other

(B) B is the most preferred

(C) B and C are within 10% of each other

(D) C is the most preferred

Votes	A	B	C
1st preference	13	54	33
2nd preference	24	37	39
3rd preference	63	9	28

Ans.(B)

Multiply with 3 of 1st preference of A,B & C ,Similarly Multiply with 2 of 2nd pref and multiply 1 with 3rd pref and add of all A , B &C and it shows that B has the highest votes, so, B is the correct answer.

144. CSIR-NET-JUN-2019

There are two examinations, A and B in a subject which are evaluated out of 30 and 70 marks, respectively. In order to pass the course the student has to get at least 40% in total and at least 40% in B. The following are the marks of the students S_1 to S_4. The only student/s to have passed is/are

(A) S_1, S_3

(B) S_2, S_3, S_4

(C) S_1, S_2

(D) S_1

Students	A	B
S_1	12	28
S_2	10	29
S_3	16	27
S_4	05	29

Ans.(D)

40% of 30 = 12 and 40% of 70 = 28, So S1 fulfil the laid down criteria.

160

145. CSIR-NET-JUN-2019

The distribution of grades secured by students in a class is given.
What is the least possible population of the class?

	Grade	Fraction of the population
(A) 2	A	0.1
	B	0.4
(C) 8	C	0.3
(D) 10	D	0.2

(B) 4

Ans.(D)

No. of students should be full no. i.e, if answer is (A) then Grade A have 0.2,

, if it is (B) then it will be 0.4,…… , if it is (C) then it will be 0.8 ,…….but if answeris(D), then No. of Students of grade A will be 1, grade B will be 4, grade Cwill be 3 and grade D will be 2, which are perfect number .

146. **CSIR-NET-JUN-2019 (Pic is not clear to give answer)**

The graph depicts the petrol prices (in Rs. Per litre) for the months April, May and June. Pick the INCORRECT statement

(A) The highest price never crossed 75

(B) The largest difference between the highest and lowest price was for the month of June.

(C) Month of June showed the largest decrease of price between the opening date and closing data price

(D) All depicted prices lie between 70 and 80

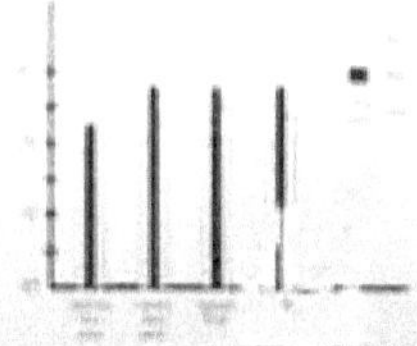

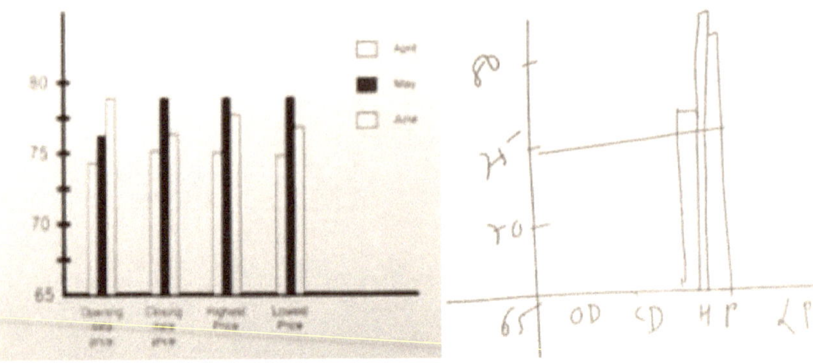

Ans.A

147. CSIR-NET-DEC-2018

Percentage-wise distribution of all science students in a university is given in the pie-diagram. The bar chart shows the distribution of physics students in different sub-areas, where a student takes one and only one sub-area. What percentage of the total science students is girls studying quantum mechanics

A 10 **B** 1 **C** 0.2 **D** 2

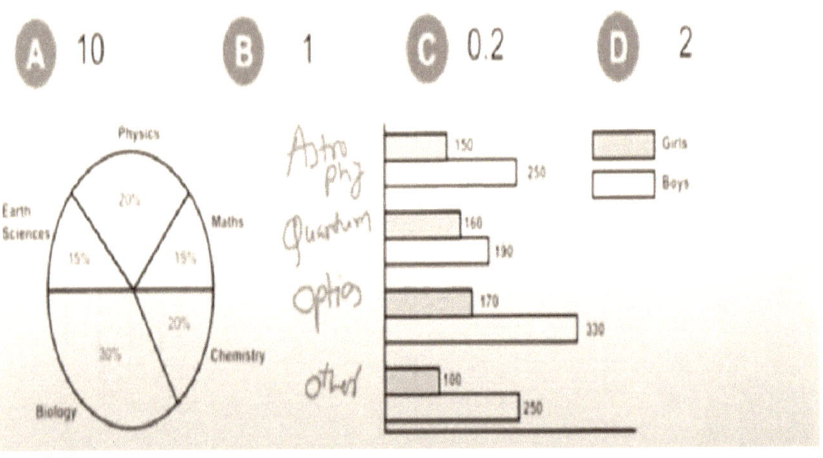

Ans.(D)

Total No. of Physics Students = 150+250+160+190+170+330+100+250=1600 ,

Now 20% students are Physics Students and the total Physics students are 1600

, Total Students will be (100/20)*1600 = 8000, The girl studying quantum mechanics are 160. So the required % = (160/8000)*100 =2

148. CSIR-NET-DEC-2018

Election results of a city, which contains 3 segments (A, B and C) are given in the table. Percentage votes obtained by parties X, Y and Z are also shown. Which party won the election?

Segment	Total Voters	% of voting	X	Y	Z
A	2 00 000	60	30	30	40
B	2 50 000	70	40	30	30
C	3 00 000	80	30	40	30

(A) Y

(B) X

(C) Z

(D) It was a tie between X and Y

Ans.(A)

Seg me nt	Total Voters	% of voti ng	Total Casted Votes	X		Y		Z	
A	200000	60	120000	30%	36000	30%	36000	40%	48000
B	250000	70	175000	40%	70000	30%	52500	30%	52500
C	300000	80	240000	30%	72000	40%	96000	30%	72000
					178000		**184500**		172500

149. Coordinates of a point x, y, z space is (1, 2, 3). What would be the coordinates of its reflection in a mirror along the x – z plane? (CSIR-NET-JUN-2014)

a) (-1, 2, 3)   b) (1,-2,-3)   **c)(1,-2,3)**   d)(-1,2,3)

Here , the value of y axis will be negative bur x and z axis will be positive.

150. Three identical equilateral triangular plates of side 5 cm each are placed together such that they form a trapezium. The length of the longer of the longer of the two parallel sides of this trapezium is ? CSIR-NET-JUN-2014

a) $5\sqrt{¾}$ cm   b) $5\sqrt{2}$ cm   **c) 10 cm**   d)$10\sqrt{3}$ cm

151. CSIR-NET-JUN-2018

The distribution of marks of students in a class is given by the following chart. If 3.30 marks is the passing score in a 10-mark question paper, which of the following is false?

A. Majority of the students have scored above the pass mark

B. Mode of the distribution is 3

C. Average marks of passing students is above 55%

D. Average marks of the students who have failed is below 20%

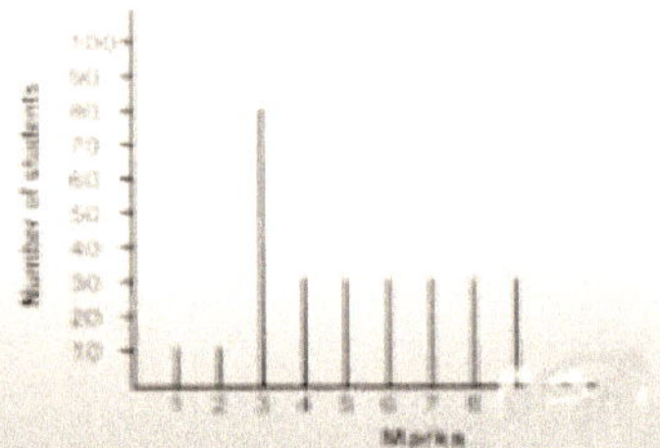

Ans.(D)

Maximum is the mode which is 3 | Pass Students = 30*(4+5+6+7+8+9) =30*39= 1170, Average Marks = 30*39/30*6=39/6=6.5 = (6.5/10)*100=65% which is above 55% | Failed Students: 10*1 + 10*2 +80*3 =270, Average Marks = 270/10+10+80 =270/100=2.7=(2.7/10)*100=27% which is above 20%

152. CSIR-NET-JUN-2018

The prices of diamonds having a particular colour and clarity are tabulated : How many 0.25 carat diamonds can be purchased for the price of a 2 carat diamond?

A. 8   B. 16

C. 32   D. 64

Weight of diamond (in carats)	Price of diamond (in Rs./carat)
0.25	1 lakh
0.5	2 lakh
1	4 lakh
2	8 lakh

Ans.(D)

Cost	Wt. of Diamond incarats	Price(In Rs./carats)
25000	0.25	1 lakh
100000	0.50	2 lakh

| 400000 | 1 | 4 lakh |
| 1600000 | 2 | 8 lakh |

25000 * X =1600000, X =1600000/25000=64

153. CSIR-NET-JUN-2017

The bar chart shows number fo seats won by four political parties A. B. C and D. Which party won the largest proportion of seats it contested?

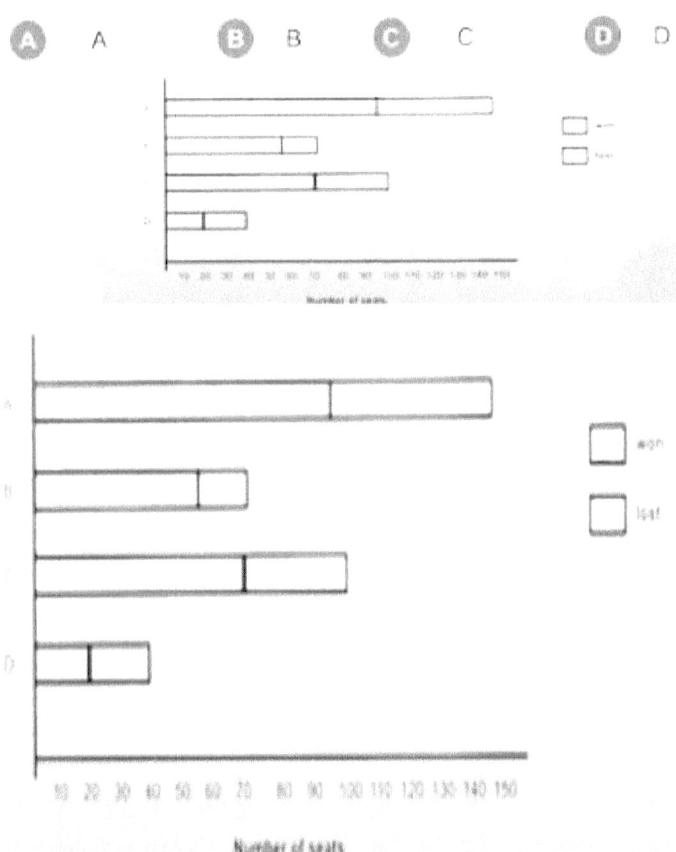

Ans.(B)

A	B	C	D
OWN 100 LOSS 50	OWN 60 LOSS 15	OWN 75 LOSS 25	OWN 20 LOSS 20

165

100/50 =2	60/15 =4	75 /25 =3	20 /20 =1

154. CSIR-NET-JUN-2017

The graph shows cumulative frequency % of research scholars and the number of papers published by them. Which of the following statements is true?

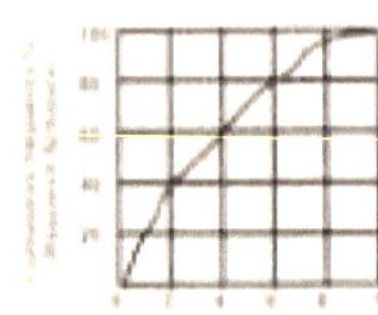

A   Majority of the scholars published more than 4 papers.

B   60% of the scholars published at least 2 papers.

C   80% of the scholars published at least 6 papers.

D   30% of scholars have not published any paper.

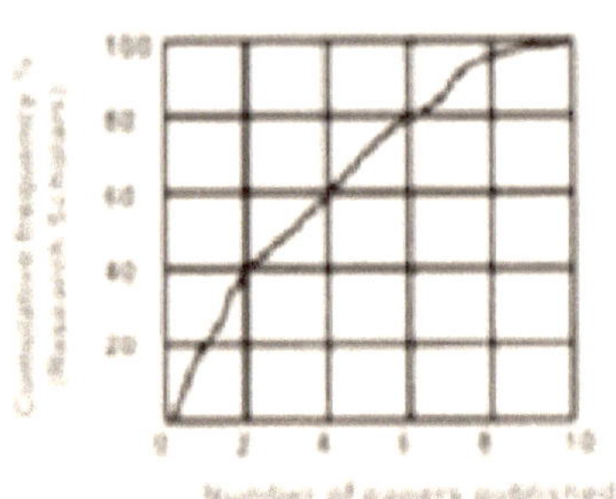

Ans.(B)

X- Number of paper published   Y – Percentage of Scholars

0 - 2	0 - 4	0 - 6	0 - 8	0 - 10
40	60	80	98	100

155. CSIR-NET-JUN-2017

Pre-PhD exam score of 10 students are plotted against their M.Sc. marks. Which of the following is true?

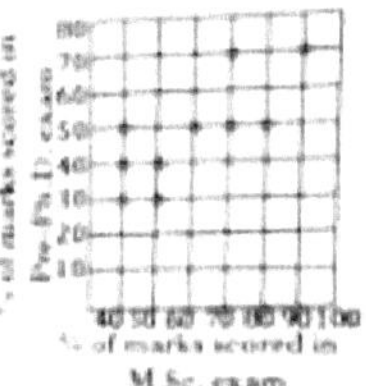

(A) Two students have scored better in Pre-PhD than their M.Sc. Exam

(B) All those students who scored 50% in Pre-PhD, score more percentage of marks in their M.Sc. exam

(C) Two students score the same percentage of marks in their Pre-PhD and M.Sc. exams.

(D) The student who scored maximum in M.Sc. is the only student to get maximum in Pre-PhD exam.

Ans. (C)

From Graph , It is seen that (A) is False , (B) is False , (C) is True and (D) is False

156. CSIR-NET-DEC-2019

Year-wise yield in science of a product is given in the graph below. Which year had the largest percent variation in the yield compared to the previous year?

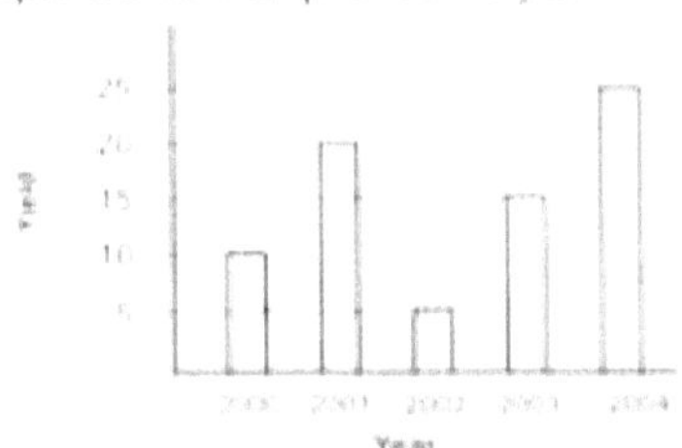

(a) 2004   (b) 2003   (c) 2002   (d) 2001

Ans.(C)

2000-2001	2001-2002	2002-2003	2003-2004
10-20	20-5	5-15	15-25
(20/10)*100= 200	(5/20)*100= 25	(15/5)*100= 300	(25/15)*100= 166

157.CSIR-NET-DEC-2016

Based on the distribution of surface area of the Earth at different elevations and depths (with reference to sea-level) shown in the figure, which of the following is FALSE?

(A) Largest proportion of the Earth is below sea-level.

(B) Of the surface area above sea-level, larger proportion lies below 2 km elevation.

(C) Of the surface area below sea-level, smaller proportion lies below 4 km depth.

(D) Distance from sea level to the maximum depth is greater than to the maximum elevation.

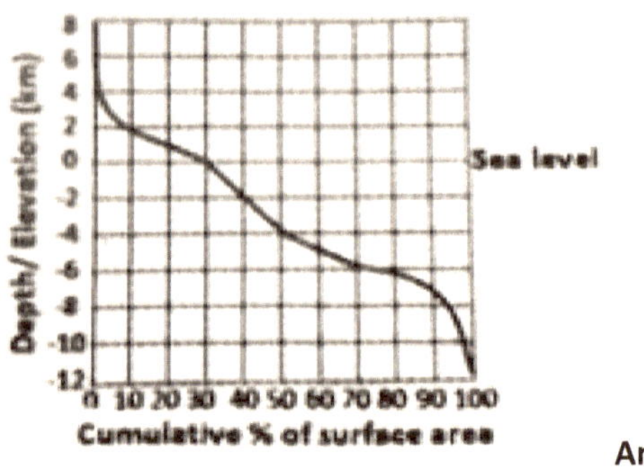

Ans.(C)

From Graph , It is seen that (A) is True , (B) is True , (C) is False and (D) is True

158. CSIR-NET-DEC-2016

The bar chart shows number of seats won by four political parties in a state legislative assembly. Which of the following pie-charts correctly depicts this information

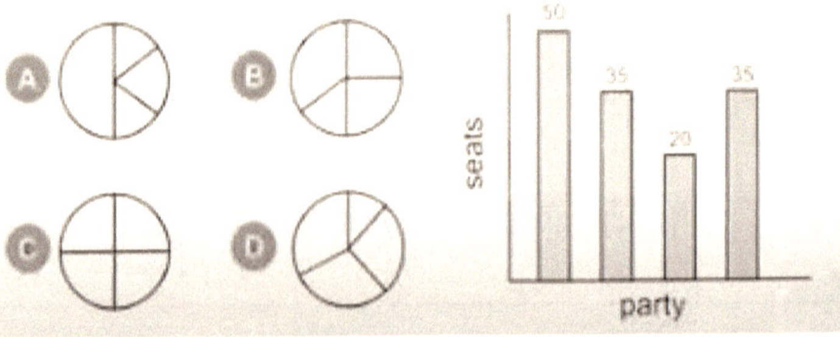

Ans.(B)

Total seats won = 50 + 35 + 20 + 35 =140 , The % of seats are (50/140)*100 = 35.7% ,(35/140)*100 = 25%, (20/140)*100 = 14.3% and (35/140)*100 = 25%, So the Pie Chart distribution will be 35,25 ,25 ,15.

159. CSIR-NET-JUN-2016

The function f(x) is plotted against x as shown. Extrapolate and find the value of the function at x = -1

A. -0.01

B. -0.1

C. 0.01

D. 0.1

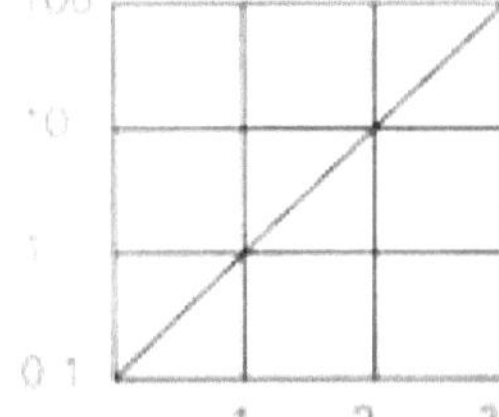

Ans.(C)

$f(1)=1$, $f(2)=10=10^1$, $f(3)=100=10^2$, $f(x)=10^{x-1}$ if x=-1 then $f(-1)=10^{-1-1}=10^{-2}=1/100=.01$

160. CSIR-NET-JUN-2016

An experiment leads to the following set of observations of the variable v at different times t.

t	0	1	2	3	4	5	6
v	5	6.1	9.1	13.7	20.6	30.8	41.4

Allowing for experimental errors, which of the following expressions best describes the relationship between t and v?

A. $v \propto t$

B. $(v - 5) \propto t$

C. $v = 5t + t^2$

D. $(v - 5) = (t + 5)^2$

Ans.(B)

Option (A) is not true, because $5 \propto 0^2$ is not possible. Option (B) – if we deduct 5 from v then v will be 0.

161. CSIR-NET-DEC-2016

Wheat production of a country over a number of years is shown. Which year recorded highest percent reduction in production over the previous year?

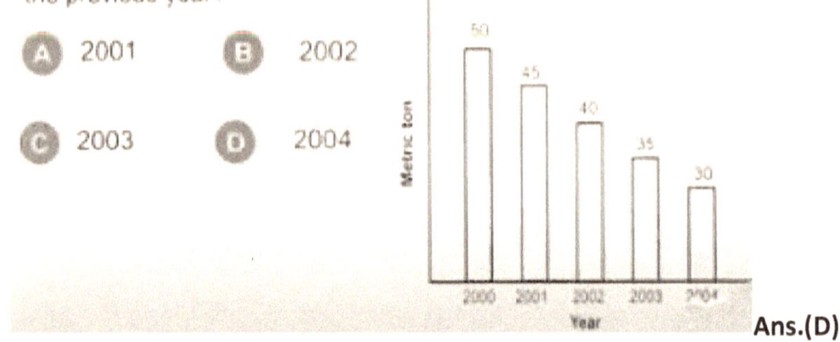

A. 2001

B. 2002

C. 2003

D. 2004

Ans.(D)

Reduction : 2000-2001 --(50-45)/50 * 100 =10% | 2001-2002--(45-40)/45 * 100 =11.11% AND 2002-2003--(40- 35)/40 * 100 =12.50% | 2003-2004--(35- 30)/35 * 100 =14.28%

162. CSIR-NET-JUN-2015

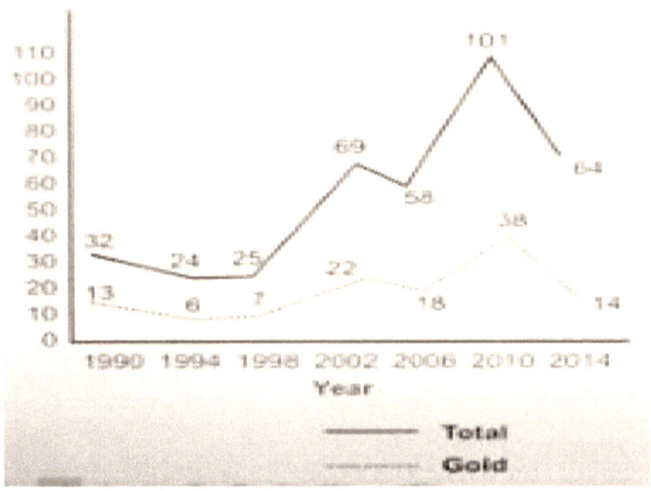

Based on the graph, which of the following statements is NOT true?

A. Number of gold medals increased whenever total number of medals increased

B. Percentage increase in gold medals in 2010 over 2006 is more than the corresponding increase in total medals.

C. Every time non-gold medals together account for more than 50% of the total medals.

D. Percentage increase in gold medals in 2010 over 2006 is more than the corresponding increase in 2002 over 1998.

Ans.(D)

Option D: 2002 over1998 – (15/7)*100 = 214%   2010 over 2006 = (20/18)*100=111%

163. CSIR-NET-DEC-2014

The following graphs depict variation in the value of Dollar and Euro in terms of Rupee over six months. Which of the following statements is TRUE?

A. Values of Dollar and Euro rose steadily from January to June

B. Values of Dollar and Euro rose by equal rate between January to March

C. The rise in the value of Dollar from April to May is three times the fall in Euro during the same period.

D. Values of Dollar and Euro rose equally between May and June

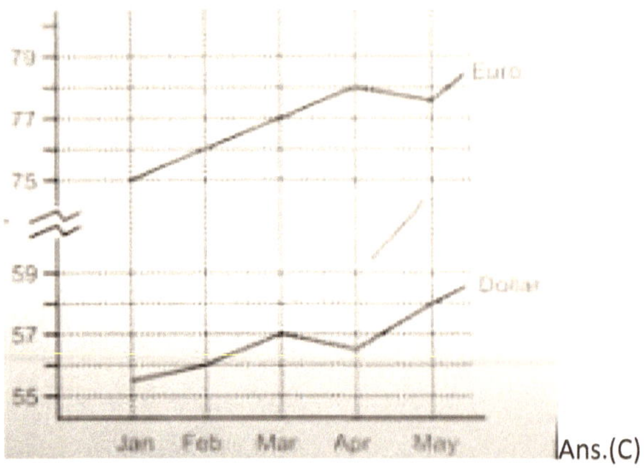

Ans.(C)

A) If rose steadily then both the graph should be straight line, which is not true

B) Dollar increase between January to March → 57 – 55.5 =1.5 and Euro →77-75 =2 ,So it is not true.

C) Rise of Dollar from April to May = 58 - 56.5 =1.5 Fall in Euro from April to May =78 – 77.5 =.5 which is true.

164. CSIR-NET-DEC-2014

Average yield of a product in different years is shown in the histogram.
If the vertical bars indicate variability during the year, then during
which year was the percent variability over the average of the year
least?

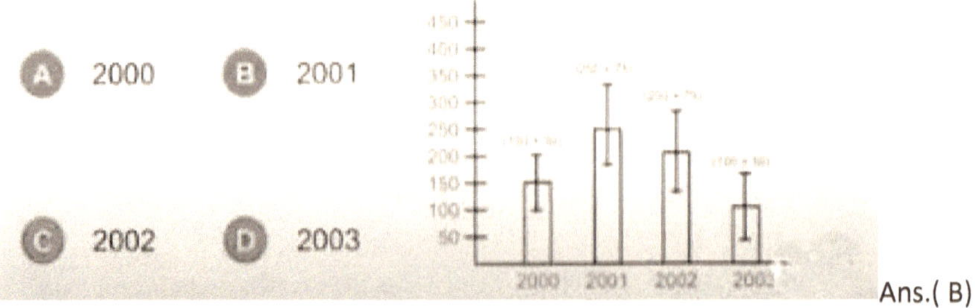

A) 2000 B) 2001

C) 2002 D) 2003

Ans.(B)

Variability in 2000→ (50/150)*100 = 33% ; Variability in 2001→ (75/250)*100 = 30%; Variability in 2002→ (75/200)*100 = 37%;
Variability in 2003→ (50/100)*100 = 50% , So , the least variation is 30% -- The correct answer is (B).

165. CSIR-NET-JUN-2014

Marks obtained by two students S1 and S2 in a four-semester course are plotted in the following graph. Which of the following statements is true?

(A) S2 got higher marks than S1 in all four semesters.

(B) Over four semesters. S1 improved by a higher percentage compared to S2

(C) Total marks of S1 and S2 are equal

(D) S1 and S2 did not get the same marks in any semester.

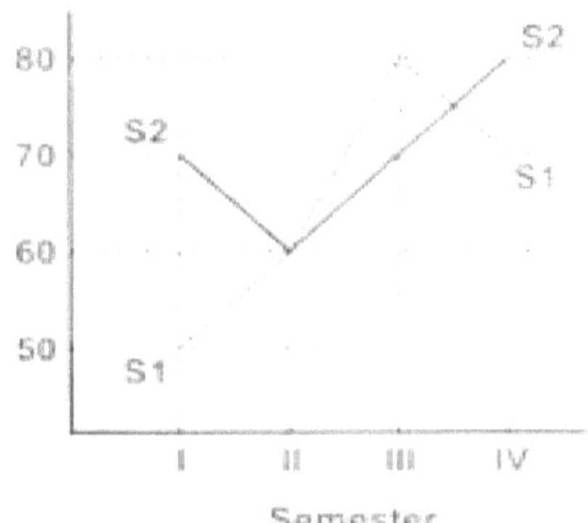

S1	S2
50	70
60	60
80	70
70	80
260	280

Ans. (B)

A) In Third sem S1 got Higher marks than S2(S1→ 80 and S2→70   B) S1 =(20/50)*100 = 40%   S2 = (10/70)*100=14%   C) S1 =260 and S2 = 280

166. CSIR-NET-JUN-2016

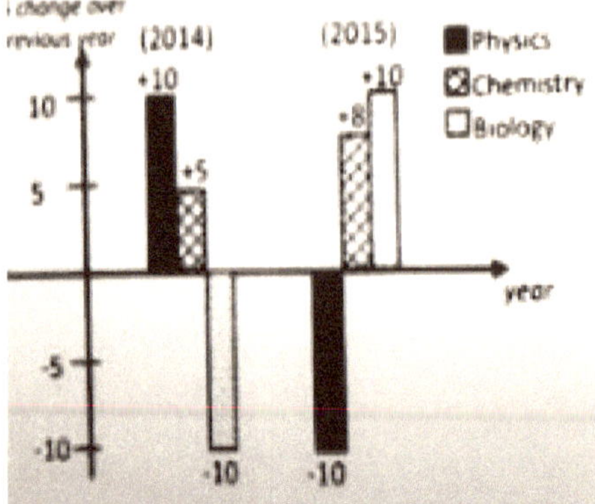

Which of the following inferences can be drawn from the graph?

A. The total number of students qualifying in Physics in 2015 and 2014 is the same.

B. The number of students qualifying in Biology in 2015 is less than that in 2013.

C. The number of Chemistry students qualifying in 2015 must be more than the number of students who qualified in Biology in 2014.

D. The number of students qualifying in Physics in 2015 is equal to the number of students in Biology that qualified in 2014.

Ans. (B)

Let there is 100 students pass in 2013, In 2014 physics students pass is 110 and in 2015 the physics students pass will be 110- 110*10/100 =100-11=89 , Which is not same.

Let there is 100 students pass in 2013, In 2014 Biology students pass is 90 (100-10/100*100) and in 2015 the Biology students pass will be 90 + (10/100)*90 =99 , Which is true.

www.ingramcontent.com/pod-product-compliance
Lightning Source LLC
Chambersburg PA
CBHW031114250726
48655CB00004B/1712